"A must-read for anyone looking to retire comfortably...Lichtenfeld provides unique ideas that will literally put thousands of dollars in your bank account starting right now."

—**Frank Curzio**,
President and CEO, Curzio Research

"Every investor who wants to live life on his or her terms needs to read this book. It's clearly written, easy to understand and filled with profitable advice - in plain English."

—**Keith Fitz-Gerald**,
Chief Investment Strategist,
MoneyMorning.com and Money Map Press

"Marc's book of creative ideas for building income and accumulating wealth is a godsend for retirees today. This book is a must-read!"

—**Zach Scheidt**,
Agora Financial

You Don't Have to Drive an Uber in Retirement

You Don't Have to Drive an Uber in Retirement

HOW TO MAINTAIN YOUR LIFESTYLE WITHOUT GETTING A JOB OR CUTTING CORNERS

Marc Lichtenfeld

WILEY

For general information on our other products and services or for technical support, please contact our Customer Care Department within the United States at (800) 762-2974, outside the United States at (317) 572-3993, or fax (317) 572-4002.

Wiley publishes in a variety of print and electronic formats and by print-on-demand. Some material included with standard print versions of this book may not be included in e-books or in print-on-demand. If this book refers to media such as a CD or DVD that is not included in the version you purchased, you may download this material at http://booksupport.wiley .com. For more information about Wiley products, visit www.wiley.com.

Library of Congress Cataloging-in-Publication Data:

Names: Lichtenfeld, Marc, author.
Title: You don't have to drive an Uber in retirement : how to maintain your
   lifestyle without getting a job or cutting corners / by Marc Lichtenfeld.
Description: Hoboken, New Jersey : John Wiley & Sons, Inc., [2017] | Includes
   index. |
Identifiers: LCCN 2017057205 (print) | LCCN 2017059020 (ebook) | ISBN
   9781119347187 (pdf) | ISBN 9781119347163 (epub) | ISBN 9781119347149
   (cloth)
Subjects: LCSH: Retirement income. | Retirees—Finance, Personal. |
   Retirement.
Classification: LCC HG179 (ebook) | LCC HG179 .L4853 2017 (print) | DDC
   332.024/014—dc23
LC record available at https://lccn.loc.gov/2017057205

Cover Design: Wiley
Cover Image: © ICHIRO/Getty Images

Printed in the United States of America.

10 9 8 7 6 5 4 3 2 1

To Mom and Dad.

Thank you for your love, support, and for leading by example.

Contents

Foreword

By Mark Skousen
Editor, *Forecasts & Strategies*

> *"An investment in knowledge pays the best interest."*
>
> *– Ben Franklin*

Although I have not retired yet – I'm still teaching economics, writing an investment newsletter, and speaking at conferences – I'm concerned, like all of you, that my wife and I have enough to live on when and if we decide to retire.

I also just signed up for Social Security, so I'm glad to see that apparently I made the right choice, according to Marc Lichtenfeld. Among the many tips he provides in his excellent, comprehensive study, he suggests that if you wait until the optimal time, you'll get 8% more per year compared to what you'll get paid if you sign up at an earlier time. If you live to the average lifespan, you will be ahead by thousands. Moreover, retirees are active and living longer, so you will be even more ahead.

What is the key to successful retirement when defined as maintaining a fulfilling lifestyle in your mature years? Stay active and healthy, exercise, play sports, eat right, socialize a lot with family and friends, meet new friends, keep learning, do volunteer work, be involved in your community, run for office, attend church or other religious/spiritual activities, read books and newspapers, check your email, text your friends; but don't spend all your time watching TV, playing video games, or hitting a white ball around the green hills of America every day. Diversify!

That's quite a laundry list, but the whole idea is to keep your mind, body, and soul lively and engaged.

Despite the title, Lichtenfeld is not against working in retirement. He makes a point that you may want to have a part-time job, but it should be voluntary: "You don't have to drive for Uber, but you may want to." Retirement can get boring fast if you don't have something engaging to do.

Lichtenfeld shows a variety of other ways to boost your income in retirement, beyond your pension and Social Security checks. You should have an investment account with a brokerage firm, including an individual retirement account (IRA) or 401k plan. He shows you how to increase your income by switching to high-quality companies that pay a high and rising dividend, what he calls "Perpetual Dividend Raisers." I call it the SWAN strategy: Sleep Well at Night! Don't miss that section.

In fact, you may want to read another one of his books called *Get Rich with Dividends*. And you may want to subscribe to his newsletter, *The Oxford Income Letter*, to keep current and find new ways to invest.

He also writes about using put and call options in a conservative way to earn more monthly income. And that's not all: He gives you sound advice when being tempted to earn more money by loaning money to family members, lending funds to friends and neighbors, and buying tax liens.

Speaking of loaning money to relatives, I was once approached by a younger brother who wanted to borrow $5,000. Instead of loaning it to him directly, together we went to a local bank, where I deposited $5,000 into a bank CD; and then the bank loaned my brother the $5,000, with a lien on the CD. This strategy increased the chances that my brother would pay off the loan, because if he didn't, it would go on his credit rating. Guess what? He paid off the loan, early!

Regarding the desire to earn more income, I would add one more word of caution: Beware of financial fraud-peddlers who promise extraordinary profits, or "guaranteed" above average returns. Watch a few episodes of *American Greed*, and you'll avoid the next Bernie Madoff scandal. Don't count on the Securities & Exchange Commission or your state securities office to protect you against fraud. If you lose your money, there is no federal fraud insurance. *Caveat emptor* – let the investor beware.

Also, be sure to diversify. Don't put all your eggs in one basket. Never forget: In your youth, you want to concentrate your business interests and make a lot of money; when you are older, you want to diversify to preserve your principal.

A lot of retirees focus solely on their income and making sure they have enough to enjoy life. But as Lichtenfeld shows, you should also watch your expenses and cut the cost of living without cutting your standard of living.

The last half of the book is as important as the first half. It's all about "cutting costs" and looking for bargains when it comes to Medicare, life and medical insurance, taxes, buying a car, traveling for less, staying at hotels, going on cruises, and so on. Remember the words of Erasmus: "Frugality is a handsome income." And Seneca, who said, "Economy is a great source of revenue."

Following Marc Lichtenfeld's advice, you might end up like Arkad in *The Richest Man in Babylon*. The author George Clason writes, "In old Babylon there once lived a certain very rich man named Arkad. Far and wide he was famed for his great wealth. Also was he famed for his liberality. He was generous with his charities. He was generous with his family. He was liberal in his own expenses. But nevertheless each year his wealth increased more rapidly than he spent it."

I would offer one word of caution. Don't become a miser in your old age, where you are too conservative when it comes to spending money or going on vacations. Remember, two of the hardest things to do in life are to save when you are young, and spend when you are old. Learn balance in life. Don't be a spendthrift, but don't be a miser either.

You Don't Have to Drive an Uber in Retirement will show you how to do it without cutting corners, all the while maintaining or even boosting your lifestyle.

Good luck!

About Mark Skousen

Mark Skousen is the editor of *Forecasts & Strategies*, an investment newsletter published since 1980; the Benjamin Franklin Presidential Professor at Chapman University; and the author of *The Maxims of Wall Street*. For more information, go to www.markskousen.com.

Introduction

I'm sitting here nursing another sore calf. I went running earlier today, and my calf tightened up for the third time this week. As my grandmother used to say, "The ol' gray mare ain't what she used to be."

It wasn't that long ago that I'd suffer an athletic injury and be fine in a day or two. But now that I'm older, it takes longer to heal.

That got me thinking that I'm closer to the next stage of my life – retirement. Look at me, I'm already talking about my health problems, so I'm halfway there!

The goal of this book is to help you take control of your retirement. I'm going to show you how to increase your income and lower your costs – without negatively affecting your lifestyle.

It's unfortunate that a book like this is necessary for most retirees and pre-retirees. But the fact is, your retirement will not be the same as your parents' retirement.

First of all, we're living longer and – in many cases – healthier lives. That means we're more active and more likely to spend money doing things we enjoy, such as going out with friends, pursuing hobbies, or traveling.

Secondly, many of our parents had pensions. Today, very few of us do. And Social Security isn't going to cover all of our costs. And don't forget the children. We always say we don't want to be a burden to our children, but our adult children are an increasing burden on us.

Today, one in three 18- to 34-year olds lives with their parents.[1] It is the most common living arrangement for that age group.

Unless Junior is chipping in for groceries and other things that he uses, that's a further drain on the parents' finances.

---

[1] http://www.pewsocialtrends.org/2016/05/24/for-first-time-in-modern-era-living-with-parents-edges-out-other-living-arrangements-for-18-to-34-year-olds.

Things are rough for many retirees and pre-retirees right now. But this book will provide some solutions to get you on track and keep you there.

And you won't have to drive an Uber to do so.

The Retirement Crisis

You've probably heard the statistic by now: 10,000 boomers are turning 65 every day. But how many of them are financially prepared for retirement and know how much money they need?

Recent research indicates that Americans are dreadfully underprepared.

And it's not just people who are approaching their golden years.

According to the Federal Reserve's 2014 Survey of Household Economics and Decisionmaking, 31% of non-retirees have no retirement savings; and nearly 25% of those aged 45 or older have not saved a dime.[2]

And 47% of respondents said they could not pay for a medical emergency costing $400 or more without selling something or borrowing money.

Another survey, this one by the Economic Policy Institute, showed nearly half of all families have no retirement savings at all. Households with people aged 56 to 61, just a few years before retirement age, have a median retirement account of $17,000.[3]

The Employee Benefit Research Institute and Greenwald Associates reports that 57% of retirees have less than $25,000 in savings and investments, not including their homes and pensions. Twenty-eight percent have less than $1,000.

This is terrifying.

That means there are millions of people who will either be living on Social Security alone or will have to continue working well into their senior years. In fact, 45% of all respondents said they expect to work in retirement – which doesn't sound like retirement at all.

---

[2]http://www.federalreserve.gov/econresdata/2014-report-economic-well-being-us-households-201505.pdf.

[3]http://www.latimes.com/business/hiltzik/la-fi-mh-six-charts-on-the-retirement-crisis-20160302-column.html.

According to AARP, currently only 19% of seniors are working.[4] So the gap between those who expect to work and those who have jobs is wide.

That suggests that it may be tough for seniors to find work. It's likely one of the reasons that seniors are increasingly signing up to drive for Uber or other types of "freelance" jobs.

If you're not familiar with Uber, it's a ride service, like a taxi that you order from an app. Drivers are freelancers and work when they choose to. I cover Uber in greater detail in Chapter 6.

But I chose *You Don't Have to Drive an Uber in Retirement* as the title of this book to emphasize that if you follow the steps in this book, you won't have to be one of the nearly half of all Americans that will need to work in "retirement."

Many of the people who are not prepared for retirement worked hard their whole lives and took care of their families, but simply did not save enough for retirement or had investments wiped out.

Take Tom Palome, for example. At one time, the former vice president of marketing for Oral-B was earning $120,000 per year. He put his kids through college, helped his parents financially, and was living the American dream.

But he never saved for retirement.

When *Bloomberg Businessweek*[5] tracked him down in 2013, the then-77-year-old Palome was flipping burgers for minimum wage at a golf club. His shift ends with him mopping the floor.

Pension? What's a Pension?

You're mistaken if you believe that you're all set and don't need to save much for retirement if you have a pension. Along with a retirement crisis, there is a very real pension crisis.

Citigroup estimates there is an $18 trillion shortfall in American pensions.[6] That's *trillion*, with a T.

---

[4]https://www.washingtonpost.com/business/get-there/a-retirement-crisis-when-your-career-doesnt-last-as-long-as-you-expect/2016/03/11/116b2a46-e55a-11e5-b0fd-073d5930a7b7_story.html.

[5]http://www.bloomberg.com/news/articles/2013-09-23/why-100-000-salary-may-yield-retirement-flipping-burgers.

[6]http://www.realclearmarkets.com/articles/2016/04/04/your_retirement_dream_may_require_working_much_longer_102093.html.

For example, the city of Philadelphia owes 64,000 past and current employees $10.5 billion. It currently has $4.8 billion of it.[7]

Two major pensions for workers in the city of Chicago are currently expected to run out of cash in the next decade. Some speculate this crisis could bankrupt the city.[8]

And as I write, the Central States Pension Fund is considering cutting Teamsters' pensions by 65%.[9]

It used to be that you worked for a company or government agency for 25 or 30 years, retired, and lived happily ever after, knowing that your income and healthcare would be taken care of until you die.

That is not the case anymore for many retirees.

In 1975, more than 55% of all workers had pensions.[10] In 2011, only 3% of workers had a defined benefit pension plan with no contribution required by the worker. Another 31% contributed to their pension plan.[11]

I can count on one hand the number of friends or relatives my age or younger that have pensions. They all work for the government.

When my father retired after 35 years in the Yonkers, New York, public school system, we had a conversation that clearly illustrates the difference in expectations between his generation and mine.

Dad: I'll have to get used to living on just 75% of my income.

Me: Wait, you get paid 75% of your salary every year in retirement? That's fantastic!

Dad: Yeah, but it's less than I'm used to making.

Me: But you're not working and you're getting 75% of what you were making.

Dad: Right, but it's still less.

Me: But you're not working and you're getting 75% of what you were making when you got up early and worked all day.

It went on like that for several minutes.

---

[7]http://www.cnbc.com/2016/02/19/philadelphias-57-billion-quiet-crisis.html.

[8]http://chicago.suntimes.com/politics/ill-supreme-court-strikes-down-rescue-plan-for-2-chicago-pension.

[9]http://www.detroitnews.com/story/opinion/2016/01/05/hoffa-congress-must-act-avert-pension-crisis/78338988.

[10]http://www.accounting-degree.org/retirement.

[11]https://www.ebri.org/publications/benfaq/index.cfm?fa=retfaq14.

His generation was told that if you worked hard, your employer and the government will take care of you in retirement. And for many people that's exactly what happened.

I knew he had a pension but was stunned it would replace so much of his income. As fantastic as my employer is, they're not paying me a penny in retirement (though they do match 50 cents on the dollar in my 401k).

And from the first day I started working and learned what that 6% tax on my paycheck was (it's now 7.7%), I have assumed that Social Security would not exist when I retire and that the tens of thousands of dollars I'll contribute over my lifetime will have been used to fund someone else's retirement.

When it comes to my retirement, I expect the government to tell me, like Willy Wonka famously said to Charlie, "You get nothing! You lose! Good day, sir!"

Source: weknowmemes.com

Maybe I'll get lucky, and in the next 20 years we'll elect leaders who are more concerned with solving difficult problems than with their own re-elections.

I'll wait for you to pick yourself up off the floor from laughing at that possibility.

Unless there is some real Social Security and pension reform, I don't see how the Feds can pay me and my peers our Social Security benefits, while they are still paying many of the baby boomers and will be for years. By the time it's my turn (I was born a few years after the end of the baby boom), the system will be broke or the government will take the money from somewhere else to pay Social Security.

Since my very first paycheck, I've assumed that I'm on my own when it comes to my retirement. No company or government will be there for me. If it turns out that I'm able to collect Social Security, that will be gravy. But I'm saving and investing as if it won't be there.

Now, I'm not preaching doom and gloom, but I'm not sure how Social Security can stay solvent when, in 2025, there will be just two workers for every retiree. That compares to 3.3 in 2010 and 16 in 1950.[12]

All of this means we have to look at retirement in a new way, to adapt to our new present and future. In the following chapters I'll share proven and simple techniques for generating income in retirement.

Some are conservative methods that work decade after decade. Others are newer and more speculative but can give you exceptional returns.

No matter your risk tolerance or timeline to retirement, this book is chock full of moneymaking ideas.

I'll also show you how to lower your costs in retirement, some in big ways and others in small ways that add up. But these methods won't negatively affect your lifestyle.

I'm not telling you to sell your house and move into a smaller one, rent out the spare bedroom, or spend your mornings clipping coupons.

Many of these ideas don't require much effort, maybe a few mouse clicks and that's all. But they can add up to big savings and – along with the income techniques in this book – can help you achieve the retirement you've always wanted.

The important thing is that you take action *now*.

If you haven't started saving and investing, it's not too late, but you need to get on it immediately. The golden years are expensive.

According to the U.S. Bureau of Labor Statistics, the average retired household spends $40,938 per year.[13]

---

[12]http://www.accounting-degree.org/retirement.

[13]http://money.usnews.com/money/retirement/slideshows/the-high-costs-of-the-retirement-dream.

The average lifetime Medicare premium costs for a healthy 65-year-old couple is $266,589. When you include other healthcare costs such as dental, vision, co-pays, and so on, that figure soars to $394,454. A 55-year-old couple retiring in 10 years will pay a whopping $463,849.[14]

As I said in my last book, *Get Rich with Dividends*, I can't force you to save. I probably can't even convince you to save. If you don't see the importance of saving money for retirement, all of the great ideas in this book are meaningless.

That's on you.

I'm not going to waste my time and yours trying to convince you to put money away. I'm sure you know how important it is and that the longer your money is invested, the more income it will generate.

I could bore you with pages and pages of charts and data showing that if you save X amount for Y years, you'll end up with Z.

So let me just tell you simply: The longer your money is invested, the more it compounds. The one-year difference in how much money you will make is much larger between years 11 and 12 than between years 5 and 6.

If you haven't yet started saving for retirement, I don't care if you're 18 years old or 68 years old. Start now. And if you've already started, save more.

How Much Do I Really Need?

In order to live well in retirement you need to make sure your income (or principal that you're drawing down) is higher than your costs.

Some retirees have no desire to cut their costs in retirement. Their attitude is they worked hard and sacrificed all of their lives and now they want to enjoy the fruits of their labor.

Others have a more practical approach and prefer to live as inexpensively as possible to reduce their financial stress.

Many are somewhere in between.

This introduction will help you determine what you plan on spending in retirement so that you have a better idea of what you need. The following chapters will help you generate more income and cut the costs on dining, entertainment, and travel while still allowing you to do those things – just cheaper.

---

[14]https://www.hvsfinancial.com/PublicFiles/Data_Release.pdf.

Healthcare

You likely won't spend more in any other category than you will on healthcare. Even if you are your doctor's favorite patient because of your healthy lifestyle, things happen as we get older – often unpredictable things. And those things can be expensive.

You may exercise five days a week and never let saturated fats past your lips. You heart and arteries may be as clear as the highway early Sunday morning. And suddenly, for absolutely no reason, your colon twists, sending you to the hospital for a very invasive surgery and long recovery time.

Sure, Medicare will cover a good chunk of your costs, but not all. And depending on which Medicare plan you're on, your out-of-pocket expenses could be substantial.

According to the Kaiser Family Foundation, the average person receiving Medicare benefits spent $4,734 out of pocket in 2010.[15] And with healthcare costs expected to rise 6.5% per year for the next decade,[16] the out-of-pocket figure is rising as well.

And if you or your spouse need to stay in a nursing home, you might as well just empty your bank account, put it in a bag, and deliver it to the nursing home's accounting office.

Medicare generally does not cover nursing home stays. If patients no longer can pay for care, they can apply for Medicaid.

This happens often. A patient will move to a nursing home while they still have assets. Once those assets are drained, Medicaid kicks in. Families often move their loved one to a nicer nursing home while there are still assets to pay for it.

If one spouse is in a nursing home and the other isn't, the independent spouse may keep half of the couple's assets, up to $119,220 (plus a monthly allowance) before Medicaid kicks in.[17]

So in other words, if a couple has $400,000 in assets and one partner needs to go to a nursing home, they will pay $280,780 out of pocket before being eligible for Medicaid.

The rules are complex, so you should call your Medicaid office for further information.

---

[15]https://www.medicareresources.org/blog/2011/07/14/medicare-out-of-pocket-costs.

[16]https://www.hvsfinancial.com/PublicFiles/Data_Release.pdf.

[17]https://www.medicare.gov/what-medicare-covers/part-a/paying-for-nursing-home-care.html.

The Fun Stuff

Presumably, you didn't work your whole life just so that you could pay doctors in your senior years. You'd like to actually have some fun.

Not always, but usually, fun costs money.

If you plan on generating $40,000 per year in income from your nest egg (not including Social Security), you'll need about $1.2 million to start with.[18] We're in a period of incredibly low interest rates, which is hurting retirees and their returns. If rates return to normal, savers will be able to get by with a smaller account.

I know, I'm painting a scary picture. But I promise you: I have techniques in the following pages that will save you hundreds or thousands of dollars per year on your "fun" expenses.

Dining Out

In 2016, restaurants boomed. While economic growth may be sluggish, the restaurant industry is anything but. In October 2016, restaurant and bar sales were up 6.1%.[19] And people are spending more on dining out then on groceries.

It's now more expensive than ever to eat out. In 2016, restaurants boosted prices by 2.8% while food prices at grocery stores have fallen nearly 2%.[20]

That's not shocking when you consider that a restaurant's costs are more than just food. Labor and rent are huge components of their operating expenses, and both categories have seen big increases over the past few years.

In fact, it now costs 20% more to dine out relative to eating in.

Currently, Americans eat out an average of 4.2 times per week.[21] Those meals cost an average of $12.75 each.[22] Keep in mind that includes a lot of fast food.

But you're not a kid anymore. You may grab a quick burger while you're running errands, but your idea of a night on the town

---

[18]http://www.aarp.org/work/retirement-planning/info-2015/nest-egg-retirement-amount.html.

[19]http://www.npr.org/sections/thetwo-way/2016/10/15/497992789/three-bits-of-business-news-you-ll-be-glad-to-know.

[20]http://www.spokesman.com/stories/2016/oct/14/lower-food-prices-seen-at-the-store-but-eating-out.

[21]http://www.thesimpledollar.com/dont-eat-out-as-often-188365.

[22]Ibid.

probably doesn't include someone saying, "Do you want to supersize that?"

Morgan Stanley did a survey of the average check per person at 22 chain restaurants ranging from the cheapest – Red Robin, which was $12.17 – to the most expensive – Eddie V's at $88.

The median was $20.05.[23]

For a couple, that's $40.10. Add in a 15% tip and you're over $46.

If the couple can cut back just one meal a week and eat at home instead, the savings can be significant.

Let's assume it will cost $4 per person to eat at home. That would be a savings of $38 per week or $1,976 per year. Would you be willing to miss one trip to The Cheesecake Factory per week in order to put $1,976 per year in your pocket?

If you're like the average American, you'd still be eating out three times per week, but now would have an extra $1,976.

But this book isn't about admonishing you to stay home eating canned soup and toast and watching Seinfeld reruns when you'd rather be out with friends or a special someone.

Sure you can save money by cutting back, but later on I'll show you ways you can save money on dining and how you can even get cash back or other rewards.

Travel

Some retirees' or future retirees' idea of a perfect retirement is jetting around the world, taking luxurious cruises, or traveling the country in an R.V. – finally getting the time to travel, see things and places they've always wanted to see, and visit the kids and grandkids.

It's hard to determine what the "average" retiree will spend on travel because what is an "average" retiree? With blended families and adult children (or parents) moving away, the average retiree may find themselves on the road more than they planned in order to get some cuddle time with the grandkids.

If you're fortunate to live near your loved ones, then your travel budget may include dream vacations such as a road trip to U.S. National Parks or a European cruise.

But if your family lives in another state, you may find yourself battling other weary travelers every Thanksgiving and Christmas.

---

[23] http://www.businessinsider.com/how-much-it-costs-to-eat-at-restaurants-2015-3.

There are plenty of ways to get discounts or even free travel that don't require you to sail on a freighter. We'll go over these strategies a bit later.

Now that you have a rough idea of what you may need to spend on certain categories, it's important to understand several methods for tapping into your retirement funds.

Withdraw too quickly, and the money could run out. Go too slowly, and you may be depriving yourself of some of life's pleasures.

The 4% Rule

The 4% rule has been around for a few decades. It enables you to withdraw funds while the rest of your money grows.

It's simple. You withdraw 4% of your savings per year. If you want to maintain your buying power, you add 2% to the total. So, if you are withdrawing $25,000 in year one, the next year you take out $25,500. That extra 2% helps keep up with inflation, but obviously drains your account faster.

The idea is that withdrawing 4% of your funds per year, assuming average annual total returns on the remaining funds, should last about 30 years.

70% to 80% Rule

Other conventional wisdom suggests that retirees should plan on needing 70% to 80% of their pre-retirement income to live comfortably.

But that figure has been challenged in recent years as some costs are eliminated in retirement.

Though I won't talk about it in this book, some retirees downsize their home, lowering their housing costs. I don't see anything wrong with doing that. In fact, it makes sense. But the idea of this book is to provide techniques that won't force you to radically alter your life.

Other costs associated with work, such as commuting, lunches, and professional organization memberships, mostly disappear in retirement.

According to a T. Rowe Price survey, retirees said they needed 66% of their pre-retirement income to live as well or better than they did while they were working.[24]

---

[24]http://www.kiplinger.com/article/retirement/T037-C000-S004-replace-80-of-preretirement-paycheck.html.

What's In This Book?

As I mentioned, this book is full of ideas for generating income, saving money, and turning that saved money into more money.

We'll start off with the income generators.

In Chapter 1, we'll focus on my favorite strategy for income, whether you're in retirement or still working. And the best part of it is you'll get a boost in income every year, which will, at the very least, keep up with inflation and in all likelihood beat the pants off inflation.

That will help you not only maintain your buying power but increase it.

We'll discuss options in Chapter 2. If you've never traded options before, don't be scared off. At least read the chapter. They're not as complicated as people think nor are they as risky – at least not the way I show you how to trade them.

Most people lose money when trading options because they swing for the fences, trying to make enormous gains. We're using a different strategy – one that will make a few percentage points every month. Add it up and annually you can generate double-digit yields on your investment capital.

It's a very conservative strategy and is one used by many of the wealthiest investors – including Warren Buffet. Make sure you read that chapter.

Chapter 3 focuses on a way you can be the bank. You can create a loan portfolio, where you are the lender. That portfolio can be as conservative as you want it to be, with only the highest-grade borrowers, or as risky as you can handle, where you'll earn exceptionally high yields, but the risk of default is higher – and everything in between.

And if you find yourself loaning money to family members, I'll show you how to protect yourself.

We'll also go over a way to generate a strong yield by providing short-term loans to homeowners or builders.

It's a great way of making your money work hard for you.

In Chapter 4, we'll talk about how you can cash in when someone else doesn't pay their taxes – and possibly get property ridiculously cheap.

Chapter 5 is an important one as I offer tips on how to maximize your Social Security. You've paid into it for all these years; you deserve every penny you can squeeze out of it. I'll show you how to do just that.

In Chapter 6, we'll discuss ways you can work in retirement to generate some extra income, but completely on your own terms. If it's a beautiful Saturday afternoon and you don't feel like working, you don't. If suddenly you find yourself with a few spare hours and nothing to do, you clock in and start making money.

Chapter 7 uncovers a new type of 401k you may not be familiar with. But if you have access to it, you won't want to miss a word on how you can add thousands of dollars to your retirement accounts, even if your regular 401k is maxed out.

Then, we switch gears and talk about some simple ways you can lower your expenses. I'll discuss simple tools and strategies that will save you thousands of dollars per year.

Chapter 8 discusses Medicare. I kick off the chapter alerting you to the most critical and easy-to-make mistake that can cost you thousands of dollars. The rest of the chapter provides steps to help you save big bucks on Medicare without sacrificing quality.

In Chapter 9, I outline how you can receive great quality healthcare at a fraction of the normal cost.

Chapter 10 helps you combat one of the most out of control costs in retirement – the constantly rising price of medicine. You'll be surprised how much you can save (or even get your medicine for free), with a free app or easy to use service.

Chapter 11 is about everyone's favorite subject – taxes. Except you'll love these strategies to keep more of your money in your pocket instead of Uncle Sam's.

I'll show you how to make your investments work harder for you in Chapter 12. The more money you keep, the more money your money makes. You can save tens of thousands of dollars over your lifetime with the ideas in this chapter.

Next, I'll show you how to cut another big expense – your car. No, I'm not going to tell you to take the bus. But the next time you buy a car, you'll save thousands of dollars if you follow the advice in Chapter 13.

And in Chapter 14, I'll show you how to cut your travel costs.

In Chapter 15, we'll go through lots of small and fun ideas that add up to big bucks both in income and savings. Any one of these ideas alone will cover the cost of this book. And if you borrowed it from the library, you're ahead of the game. And no, that's not one of my suggestions.

You'll learn about ways to save or even get cash back for shopping online, buy gift cards at discounted prices, or where to take classes on just about anything for free.

The last section of the book addresses popular strategies that are actually terrible ideas that could jeopardize your retirement and destroy your wealth.

Chapter 16 discusses the worst investment you can make. It's one that a lot of people get talked into making.

If you have life insurance or are considering getting some, you must read Chapter 17. It could help you avoid a very costly error.

Another bad idea, which is featured non-stop on TV commercials these days, is revealed in Chapter 18.

At the end of each chapter, I list a few bulleted "actions to take" that you can do to get started implementing the strategies right away.

So let's get started securing or enhancing your retirement. That way you'll have more time to listen to me gripe about my aches and pains.

PART

I

Generating Income

Make money money, make money money money!
— EPMD (an American hip-hop group)

This first section of *You Don't Have to Drive an Uber in Retirement* will show you different ways of creating new income streams.

Several will require some work but are lucrative. And you may have fun doing them.

But none require you to change your lifestyle or to put in hours when you don't want to. I'm not recommending that you get a job where you're expected to show up at a certain time on a certain day.

If any of the ideas in this section appeal to you, do them when you feel like it. If you'd rather play golf or take a snooze, no worries. These opportunities will be there tomorrow.

Of course, the more you put into these ideas, the more you'll get out of them. And I expect that you'll find these moneymaking recommendations enjoyable enough that you'll want to do several of them, especially once the register starts ringing.

But again, this book is all about maintaining your lifestyle, not drastically changing it (unless you want to).

By taking some of the actions in this section, you'll regain control over your retirement and not be as dependent on a government or corporate promise.

Having some income will relieve stress and ensure that you have enough money both to cover your bills and pay for some extras.

Let's start making money.

CHAPTER 1

Give Yourself a Raise

"The two most powerful warriors are patience and time."

– Leo Tolstoy

There are few feelings as satisfying as getting a raise. It's great to know that you're going to make more money this year than you did last year.

My first job out of college, I was paid the princely figure of $22,500 a year. I performed well in my position and when I met with my boss for my review, I was given a 5% raise to $23,625. The maximum I could have received was 6%, but I was told nobody ever gets that. (I never understood that line of thinking, but that's another issue.)

I was living in Manhattan with two roommates and barely getting by. I had a girlfriend who had expensive tastes and little income. Now, that extra $21.62 (before taxes) per week wasn't going to keep her in the lifestyle she expected to become accustomed to, but it was a little more breathing room. Not much, but a little more.

Importantly, it gave me a feeling of pride in not just knowing that my company felt I was valuable (although apparently not 6% more valuable), but that I was progressing financially.

Now that I'm older and wiser, I have set up my portfolio so that I get a big fat raise every year – bigger than the 6% that eluded me when I was just starting out.

The way I do that is with Perpetual Dividend Raisers. This is my favorite strategy for income and wealth creation whether you're in retirement already or are still working.

I not only want to see the portfolio balance moving higher, but the amount of income that is generated each year should climb too.

In retirement, that's not just a matter of convenience or pride. It may be the difference between going to a restaurant once or twice a week and eating ramen noodles.

As I outlined in the introduction, Social Security may not be there, so income from your investments will be a critical part of keeping you afloat. Even if you receive Social Security, the average monthly Social Security check of $1,341[1] doesn't exactly enable you to take the grandkids to Disney or play too many rounds of golf.

And don't think just because you have a nest egg, you're all set. One medical emergency can drain that pretty quickly.

Medical emergencies are just that, sudden, unexpected and frequently ill-timed. Shortly after he retired, my friend's father came down with a serious but treatable illness. However, his medication costs $52,260 per year out of pocket.

As I mentioned in the introduction, if you're 65 or under, you'll likely spend somewhere between a quarter of a million and half a million dollars on healthcare in the next several decades.

And those costs rise sharply every year. Until the Great Recession in 2008, healthcare costs consistently increased at least 6% per year. Since 2008, those numbers have slowed a bit, though they are still well above the inflation rate.

In 2014, healthcare costs climbed 3.4% while the consumer price index inched up 0.8%. But, by the time you read this book. the growth in cost is expected to get back to the historical 6% average.[2]

That means whatever you have stashed away in the bank or in an annuity is going to be worth less five years from now than it is today. Ten years from now you'll hardly recognize the buying power of your retirement accounts.

If healthcare returns to its 6% inflation rate, your nest egg will be worth one-third less in five years than it is today in healthcare dollars. In other words, what costs $100,000 today will cost $133,822 five years from now.

---

[1] https://faq.ssa.gov/link/portal/34011/34019/Article/3736/What-is-the-average-monthly-benefit-for-a-retired-worker.

[2] https://www.hvsfinancial.com/PublicFiles/Data_Release.pdf; http://www.pwc.com/us/en/health-industries/health-research-institute/behind-the-numbers.html.

In ten years, you'll need nearly double what you have today to buy the same healthcare goods and services. What costs $100,000 today will run you $179,084 a decade from now.

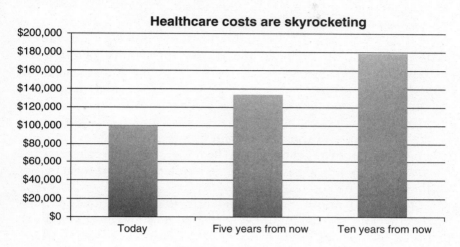

And that's just healthcare costs. That doesn't include fun things like nursing homes. It is expected that at least 40% of seniors will require nursing home care. And many others will have live-in help. Those things aren't cheap.

So it's not enough to just have a nice stash of cash. That money or, better yet, the income it spins off need to grow each year so you're dipping as little as possible into the nest egg.

Keep in mind, the less money you have, the less income it will likely generate.

It's critically important that you not only have a solid base, but that the money generates income that goes up every year. If your income grows enough, you'll actually increase your buying power, rather than just making sure you can keep up with the rising doctors' bills.

There are many ways of creating a growing and diverse income stream. We'll talk about quite a few of them in this book.

Perpetual Dividend Raisers

The easiest way that you can grow your annual income is by investing in Perpetual Dividend Raisers.

These are stocks that raise their dividends every year. I wrote extensively about this subject in my last book *Get Rich with Dividends.*

In *Get Rich with Dividends,* I outlined a strategy for investing in stocks that would generate 11% yields within 10 years or 12% average annual total returns over 10 years.

I'll go over some of the highlights here, but it's important to understand that if you need the money that you're planning on investing in stocks within three years – whether you're using this strategy or any other – you should not put it in the stock market.

Short term, too many bad things can occur. Wars start, idiots get elected (a little too frequently), recessions happen, markets crash, and a whole host of other unpleasant events take place.

You don't want to get caught in the middle of a bear market when you need the money to pay the rent. So don't invest short-term money in the market. It's too unpredictable.

Long term is another story. Long term, the market goes up. It has for over a century. You might get extended periods where not much happens like in the "lost decade" after the Great Recession – where stocks failed to go up at all when you look back at the prices from ten years earlier. It wasn't until about 2012 that investors who had been in the market for 10 years and who endured the financial crisis in 2008 were in the black again.

That's based on stock price only. It doesn't take dividends into account nor does it consider that an investor may have bought more stock when prices were falling. And if they were reinvesting dividends during the bear markets, they did even better because they were able to buy more stock, which generated more dividends, which bought more stock, which generated more dividends ...

A stock market investor should be comfortable putting his or her money to work for five years (preferably more). That way, you'll likely ride out any short-term volatility or market aberrations. The longer you can stay invested the better, as your dividends will grow and so should your capital.

So let's tackle exactly how you can extract more income from the stock market.

As mentioned earlier, Perpetual Dividend Raisers are stocks that raise their dividends every year – preferably, by a meaningful amount. They've done so for many years.

The reason a long track record is important is because it sets the bar high for management. The company has trained investors to expect a dividend raise every year. If suddenly, after 30 or 40 years of annual dividend increases, the company does not raise the dividend, management, as Ricky Ricardo might say, "has some 'splainin' to do."

If a CEO is considering not raising his company's dividend after several decades of yearly growth, he might want to make sure his LinkedIn profile and resume are up to date.

There would likely be a shareholder revolt. Not only that, the stock market would take the static dividend as a very bad sign.

A company without a track record of raising its dividend that simply maintains it will not be punished by Wall Street. But if a company that has been boosting the dividend since *Miami Vice* was popular suddenly stops increasing the dividend, the stock will likely fall – and fall hard.

The amazing thing is that, as of this writing, there are 18 companies that have raised their dividends every year for at least 50 years and six have lifted their dividends annually for 60 years.

The longest running annual dividend raising streak is American States Water (NYSE: AWR), a water utility based in San Dimas, California. The company has raised its dividend annually for an incredible 62 years. The streak started in 1955.

To put in perspective how long ago that was, 1955 was the year Marlon Brando won the Best Actor Oscar for *On the Waterfront*; "Rock Around the Clock" by Bill Haley and the Comets screamed up the Billboard charts; and more significantly, Rosa Parks refused to give up her seat on a Montgomery, Alabama, bus.

Now, don't confuse a long streak of dividend increases with a high yield. Just because a company has lifted its dividend every year doesn't mean the current yield is high (though I bet investors who bought the stock years ago are enjoying a very strong yield on their original investment).

For example, American States Water, with the longest annual dividend increase streak, only yields 2.1% as I write this. Shareholders who bought the stock ten years earlier are earning 6.1%.Twenty years prior and the yield is an astonishing 22.7% on the original investment.

If that investor had been reinvesting the dividends the whole time, the yields increase to 40.9% after 10 years and 157% after 20. By reinvesting the dividends, an investor gets one-and-a-half times his original cost paid back each year, without selling a share. That's a hell of an investment.

That's the power of compounding and reinvesting dividends, particularly with Perpetual Dividend Raisers.

You may be wondering, what does it mean to reinvest dividends?

It's quite simple. Instead of receiving a dividend check or having it deposited in your account each quarter, you use the funds from the dividend to buy more stock.

The process is done automatically. You don't have to take any action, and it doesn't cost you anything. You just have to tell your broker you want the dividends reinvested. You can choose to reinvest dividends only on specific stocks or all of the stocks in your portfolio. Just let your broker know what you prefer.

Reinvesting your dividends has many benefits.

First of all, the dividend doesn't even have to be big enough to buy a full share to be reinvested. Let's say you own 100 shares of Pfizer, which is trading at $34. It pays a quarterly dividend of $0.30 per share. So each quarter you'll receive $30.

If you called your broker or went online you wouldn't be able buy a fraction of a share with $30. Your broker won't allow it. Plus, you'd have to pay at least $7 to place the order, leaving you with just $23 to invest. But if you are automatically reinvesting dividends, you can put the entire $30 to work for you.

Your $30 dividend will buy 0.88 shares of Pfizer (30/34 = 0.88). Now, you own 100.88 shares. Next quarter your dividend payment will increase from $30 to $30.26, because of the extra 0.88 shares that you own.

If the stock was still trading at $34, you would then automatically buy 0.89 shares (30.26/34 = 0.89), bringing your total to 101.77 shares.

If the stock price stayed flat, at the end of one year you'd have 103.58 shares. After five years, you'd own 119.21 shares and your original $3,400 investment would be worth $4,053 – an increase of 19%, despite the stock price not moving a penny.

Once a decade has passed, you have 142.11 shares worth $4,831. After twenty years, you own 200 shares and have doubled your money. Again, that's assuming the stock price never budged and the dividend did not vary.

Had you simply cashed that dividend check each quarter you would have collected $2,400 in dividends. Combine that with the $3,400 value of the stock and your investment would have been worth $5,800 in total.

However, by reinvesting the dividends, the 200 shares are now worth $6,800 – a thousand dollars more.

Of course, stocks don't stay at the same price over 20 years. Heck, they usually don't stay the same over 20 seconds.

When the stock price goes up, your dividends will buy fewer shares.

Back to our original Pfizer example where that first dividend check bought 0.88 shares: What happens if the stock price goes up two points and you're reinvesting the dividend at $36 per share?

You'd buy 0.83 shares. Even though that's fewer than when the stock stayed the same, the good news is the stock price is higher, so your total investment is worth more.

But stocks don't always go up. Sometimes, they go down.

If Pfizer dipped to $32 per share, that first dividend payment would purchase 0.94 shares. That means that you're going to get a slightly higher dividend the next quarter because you have more shares – 0.94 compared to 0.88 in the original example.

Those fractions of shares can add up and put the compounding machine into overdrive.

It's why I say a bear market is a dividend reinvestor's best friend.

You might think, *how can the price of my stock going down be a good thing?*

First of all, who cares where a stock is trading unless you're planning to sell it? If you bought Pfizer because you believed it was a good value with strong fundamentals and you planned on holding it to help achieve a financial goal in ten years, would it matter where the stock is trading tomorrow? Six months from now? Or in five years?

As long as you still believed Pfizer was healthy, there would be no reason to sell its stock just because the price is lower. You don't need the money for another five years.

Again, when stocks decline, the dividend reinvestor buys more shares, which generate more dividends, which buys more shares, which generates more dividends, which buys more shares...

Let's look at an example using Pfizer once again.

Assume we hit a rough patch in the markets for the next five years, and Pfizer drops 10% per year. Ten percent per year may not sound like a catastrophe, but if the stock lost that much each year, you'd be down about 40% on your investment. Considering Pfizer is a blue chip stock, that would be a disaster.

If an investor bought 100 shares at $34 and reinvested the dividend for five years while the stock was dropping 10% per year, at the end of those five years, the original investment would only be down 5.9%. Not bad considering the stock fell 41%.

But here's the beautiful thing – those 100 shares turned into 125.2 shares because they were reinvested at a lower price.

If instead of dropping 10% per year for five years, Pfizer had climbed by the same amount as the historical market average, the investor would have ten less shares.

Of course, their stock would be worth more after five years, because the stock price would have risen over 7% per year instead of dropping 10%.

But the income generated by the stock would be higher if the stock declined because of the larger share count.

Then, when the market or stock returns to normal price behavior, the investor has more shares that rise in price and generate income.

Adding a dividend that's growing each year with a lower stock price is the best thing that can happen to you (as long as you don't need to sell). That increasing dividend will buy even more shares than it did before, allowing the investor to accumulate a larger number of shares.

Later on, you'll have more shares to sell once you need to dip into your capital. Or, if you're in the position to not have to sell any investments but can live off the income, the dividends generated will be even larger.

The Power of Compounding

Albert Einstein famously said, "Compound interest is the most powerful force in the universe." He also declared, "Compound interest is the eighth wonder of the world. He who understands it, earns it . . . he who doesn't . . . pays it."[3]

The compounding of reinvested dividends is what will help get you to where you want to be in retirement – if you have enough time to let the dividends compound.

If you're too close to retirement to let reinvested dividends compound for years but can still afford to invest in Perpetual Dividend

---

[3]http://www.quotesonfinance.com/quote/79/Albert-Einstein-Compound-interest.

Raisers, you should absolutely do so as long as you don't need the investment capital within three years.

Having those dividends increase every year will be a godsend. You'll increase your buying power as your dividends grow by more than the rate of inflation.

So if you receive $100 in dividends this year, it pays for $100 worth of goods. Next year if inflation rises to 3%, the same goods cost $103. However, because you've invested in Perpetual Dividend Raisers that raised their dividends by 8%, you receive $108, beating the pants off inflation.

The following year, inflation rises another 3%. Now the price of those original goods are $106.09. However, your dividends grew by 8% again, so your income is $116.64.

Here's a chart showing how effective compounding works in this scenario.

	Cost of goods with inflation rate: 3%	Income received with dividend growth rate: 8%
Year 0	$100	$100
Year 1	$103	$108
Year 2	$106.09	$116.64
Year 3	$109.27	$125.97
Year 4	$112.54	$136.04
Year 5	$115.91	$146.92
Year 6	$119.39	$158.67
Year 7	$122.97	$171.36
Year 8	$126.66	$185.06
Year 9	$130.45	$199.86
Year 10	$134.36	$215.84

You can see that after five years of moderate inflation, prices are more than 15% higher. However, with the 8% dividend increase each year, you're receiving 47% more income. And you have an extra $31 of buying power.

The difference gets more dramatic each year. After year 10, prices have climbed over 34%. Meanwhile your income has more than doubled. You are receiving 60% more income than needed to cover rising costs.

So even if an investor is not reinvesting the dividend, by owning stocks that raise the dividend each year by more than a few percentage points, he or she is ensuring that the income received from the investments will not only retain its buying power but will increase it.

Most retirees are hoping to simply hang on to what they have in retirement. But by investing in Perpetual Dividend Raisers, one can increase their buying power and living standards in retirement each year. For a free list of Perpetual Dividend Raisers, visit www.dripinvesting.org and click on Info/Tools/Forms. Then click on Excel Spreadsheet. There is a lot of information in the spreadsheet including the stocks' yields, the number of years they've continuously raised the dividend, financial information, and more.

If you prefer getting suggestions on which stocks to buy, check out my *Oxford Income Letter* at www.uberretirementbook.com. You'll automatically receive a $10 discount for being a reader of *You Don't Have to Drive an Uber in Retirement.*

Actions to Take

- Buy Perpetual Dividend Raisers.
- If you don't need the income right away, reinvest the dividends.
- Don't panic if the stock or the market goes down. Keep reinvesting dividends.
- Don't hold out for a 6% raise when you're entry level. You won't get it. No one does.

CHAPTER 2

Using Options for Income

"To get rich, you have to be making money while you're asleep."

– David Bailey

If you're not an experienced investor, the idea of using options might be as attractive as a day spent waiting in line at the Department of Motor Vehicles – in other words, not very.

But before you skip to the next chapter, let me show you how options can be easier than you think and generate tons of income. It's just a matter of doing them the right way: Selling, not buying them.

When most investors trade options, they speculate by purchasing calls on a stock they expect to go up or buying puts on a stock they think will go down. Most of those investors lose for a number of reasons which I'll get into.

First, a quick primer on what puts and calls are.

A put and a call are contracts to deliver shares of stock at a specific price by a specific date at the buyer's request.

A call buyer has the right, but not the obligation, to "call away," or buy, the shares from the seller at a specific price (the strike price) by a specific date (expiration).

For example, Pfizer is trading at $34 per share. A speculator buys one call contract at a strike price of $35 and January expiration.

That means the buyer can buy 100 Pfizer shares from the seller at $35, no matter where the stock is trading, at any time between now and the third Friday in January.

The Four Option Positions

Contracts are usually in 100 share lots. Expiration is usually the third Friday of the month. A few very large stocks trade "weeklies." These are options that expire every Friday of the month. But for our purposes we'll stick with regular expiration, which is the third Friday of the month.

For that right, the buyer might pay $1.05 per share or $105, since options contracts are for 100 shares at time.

Now, why in the world would a speculator pay $105 to buy 100 shares of Pfizer at $35, when they can buy them in the open market today at $34?

Perhaps they want to make sure the stock is going up before they buy it. If the stock is higher than $36.05, they will make money picking up the shares at $35 ($35 strike price + $1.05 option premium equals $36.05).

If the trade takes place in August, the buyer has five months to see if Pfizer moves higher. But they've only risked $105 instead of $3,400 to buy 100 shares. If Pfizer crashes to $20, they only lose $105, while someone who owns the stock would be down $1,400.

If Pfizer is above $35, they can call away the stock and keep the 100 shares in their portfolio. Or they can sell the call contract for a profit. If the stock is higher, the call will appreciate in price.

With Pfizer trading at $38, the call buyer could sell the calls for at least $3 ($38 − $35 = $3), nearly tripling their money.

With options, you can generate very large gains on a percentage basis with small moves in the stock price.

That's why someone would buy a call. So why would an investor sell one?

Because the buyers are usually wrong.

Most options expire worthless. The exact percentage is debatable, with some claiming that as many as 90% expire worthless. But the fact is well more than half do. Which means the seller makes money.

How?

Because if you sold that Pfizer call for $1.05, you put the $105 in your pocket. If the option expires worthless (Pfizer doesn't get to $35), nothing happens. You keep the money and your 100 shares of stock.

Selling a call on a stock that you own is known as selling a covered call. It's also referred to as a buy-write, because you buy the stock and write (sell) a covered call.

You should only sell covered calls on stocks you're okay with *selling* if they are called away.

If you plan on holding Pfizer in your account for many years as part of a dividend growth strategy as described in Chapter 1, Pfizer would not be a candidate for a covered call because you don't want to sell the stock. If the call buyer demands it, you will have to sell your Pfizer shares.

That's why I like to sell covered calls on stocks that I'm fine with owning because I think they'll go up and they pay a good dividend, but they are not stocks I expect to own for years and years.

You can sell covered calls on stocks that pay good dividends, multiplying your income. You keep the premium from the option that you sold and the dividend from the stock.

Let's stick with the Pfizer example. The company pays a quarterly dividend of $0.32 per share in March, June, September and December.

If you bought the stock in early August and sold the call, you'd collect the $105 premium and then receive $32 in dividends for every 100 shares in September. If you still owned the stock in November, you'd receive another $32.

Keep in mind that if Pfizer is above the $35 strike price, the buyer of the call could call away the stock in order to receive the dividend.

If in the third week of October, Pfizer is trading at $37, the call buyer could exercise his call, giving him your stock at $35 and the $0.32 per share dividend. You still keep the $105, plus you made $100 on the stock (you bought the 100 shares at $34).

Even if you never collected the dividend, the $205 comes out to a 6% return. You bought the stock for $3,400 ($34 × 100 shares) and made $205. A 6% return in a matter of months on a conservative stock is a heck of a return in this low interest rate environment.

And if you were able to collect one of the dividends, your income would have increased to $237, or 7% – again in just a few months.

What Could Go Wrong?

If you're potentially getting paid 6% or 7% in just a few months, there has to be some risk, right?

The risk is the same as owning a stock.

Actually, it's a little less.

If the stock crashes, you still own it. If your $34 stock slides all the way to $20, you've lost 14 points or $1,400 per 100 shares. If you sold the call, you'd have made $105, so that takes a little bite out of the shellacking; and you'd only be down $1,295 instead of $1,400, but it still hurts.

If at expiration Pfizer dropped just a little bit to $32, you've lost less than $1. You're down $2 on the stock, but kept the $1.05. So on 100 shares you're $95 in the red. You could always sell another call to capture some more income while you wait for the stock to go higher or get called away.

Of course, if you've lost confidence in Pfizer, you wouldn't want to sell a covered call on it no matter how big the premium is. Even if you could get $2 for the call, you wouldn't sell one if you weren't comfortable that Pfizer could hold its value.

So you should only sell covered calls on stocks you are comfortable with *keeping* in your portfolio.

The other risk is opportunity risk.

If you bought Pfizer at $34 and sold the January $35 call, you're obligated to sell your Pfizer shares at $35 if the call buyer demands it.

Let's say in October, Pfizer gets acquired for $50 per share. Considering Pfizer's market cap is more than $200 billion as I write this, that acquisition would be one of the largest in history . . . but humor me for a minute.

The buyer of the call could demand the stock at $35. If that happens, you keep the $105 in premium but miss out on $1,500 in gains (15 points x 100 shares).

So when you sell covered calls, you are trading potential upside for current income. You are limiting the profits you can make for guaranteed income today.

That's why you're getting paid 6% or 7% over just a few months.

Most of the time, giant stable companies don't soar 50% in a short period of time. But it can happen.

If you're selling covered calls, you know that this is an income strategy and won't second-guess yourself if the stock goes sharply higher and you miss out on some gains. That's not why you bought the stock to begin with. You bought it so you could sell a call against it. That's it. End of story.

It's like owning a store that sells lotto tickets. Sure, one of those tickets that you sold to a customer might hit, and you'll kick yourself that the winning ticket was in your possession. But that's not why you started selling lotto tickets. You sold them because they provide a nice steady income over time from the vast majority of people that don't win.

Don't Get Naked

When you own the stock and sell the call, you've sold a covered call. Some experienced traders will sell naked calls.

This isn't a trader who suddenly drops his boxers while placing a trade in his den. It's much more dangerous.

A trader who sells a naked call sells a call *without* owning the underlying stock.

If the stock falls, there's no problem. The trader keeps the options premium. But if the stock rises and the call buyer demands the stock, the seller of the call has to buy the stock in the open market to deliver it.

If the trader sold the Pfizer January $35 call for $1.05 and the stock is trading at $35.25 when the buyer demands it, no big deal. The call seller lost $0.25 per share or $25 on the transaction (bought stock at $35.25 and sold at $35), but kept the $1.05 per share or $105 per 100 shares. So she came out ahead.

But what if Pfizer is trading at $38? Now she has to buy the stock at $38 and sell it to the call buyer at $35. She still keeps the $1.05, so the total loss is $1.95 ($3 loss on the stock plus $1.05 gain on the option premium).

The real danger is if the stock soars. If Pfizer gets acquired in our make-believe mega merger, the trader has to buy the stock for $50 and sell it to the call buyer at $35, taking a big loss in exchange for a maximum gain of $1.05.

When you sell a covered call, your risk is capped by how low the stock can fall, which is to zero (minus whatever you received in premium). In our Pfizer example, the maximum loss would be $32.95 per share ($34 − $1.05). It's unlikely that Pfizer will fall to zero in such a short period of time, but it's useful to understand what the maximum risk is.

However, when you sell a naked call, your risk is unlimited. After Pfizer agrees to be acquired for $50, a bidding war breaks out and the stock marches higher to $60, then $70, then $100 and higher.

The losses keep mounting for the seller of a naked call. It's a very dangerous strategy with limited gains and unlimited risk.

If you want to sell calls, stick to covered calls. It's a conservative strategy used by some of the most successful investors on Wall Street.

Get Paid to Wait

How many times have we had an appointment with a doctor or with the cable company and waited an hour or more past our appointment time? Haven't we all fantasized about sending them a bill for our time?

In a way, you can do that in the options market.

You can get paid to wait for an overvalued stock to come down to your price.

Let's say you're a big fan of Apple (Nasdaq: AAPL). You own the latest iPhone, iPad, and MacBook. You think it's a great company and expect the new iPhone 43 to be a huge seller. The only problem is that at $100 per share you think the stock is a bit pricey.

You've done your homework and determined that while $100 is too much to pay for the stock, $90 is a fair price. At $90, you'd be comfortable buying shares of Apple.

Most investors will simply watch the stock that they desire and wait . . . and wait . . . and wait.

And if Apple never gets down to $90, they don't make any money.

You, on the other hand, are selling naked puts and are getting paid to wait.

Now, remember, I said never to sell naked *calls*. It's very dangerous. You have limited upside with unlimited risk.

Naked puts are actually a conservative strategy, but you have to be able to handle some volatility.

When you sell a naked put, you are selling a put to a buyer who is either making a bet that the stock will go down in price or is hedging their long position in the stock.

For the buyer of the put, it's like buying insurance. They participate in the upside if the stock goes higher, but if the stock slips, they are protected by the put.

A put buyer has the right but not the obligation to sell their stock to the put seller at the strike price at any time before the expiration date.

It's the opposite of a call. The call buyer has the right to *buy* stock at the strike. The put buyer has the right to *sell* stock.

The seller of the put is agreeing to purchase the stock from the put buyer. Using the insurance analogy, the put seller is like the insurance company and will pay the buyer if disaster strikes.

An owner of Apple at $100 may buy a January $95 put for $4. That means they are only willing to risk $5 per share (plus the price of the put). If Apple goes to $150, they participate in all of the upside minus the $4 per share, or $400 per contract.

However, if Apple collapses to $20, the put buyer has the right to sell the stock to the seller of the put at $95. So he will only lose $9 (bought Apple at $100, sold it at $95, and paid $4 for the put). Not too bad considering it could have been an $80 loss without the put (bought Apple at $100, sold it at $20).

As I said, the seller of the put is like an insurance company. And one thing we know about insurance companies is they make a lot of money. There are skyscrapers all over the United States named after insurance companies.

Sure, insurance companies occasionally have to pay a big claim when a natural disaster strikes, but over the long term, they make truckloads of cash.

Put sellers are the same. The underlying stock could collapse and the put seller will be obligated to buy the stock at a strike price that is now much higher than the current stock price, like in the Apple example.

So you have to be comfortable with that kind of risk, even though it rarely happens.

What's more likely to happen is that the put option expires worthless and you simply keep the cash.

If the stock does fall, you get your stock at the price you originally wanted.

That's important.

You only sell puts on stocks you're willing to own at the strike price.

If the stock hits your strike or goes lower, you may have to buy the stock.

I say "may" because the stock won't automatically be put to you unless it's at expiration.

For example, if you sold the Apple January $95 put and on December 15 Apple is trading at $90, the put buyer may not force you to buy the stock. She may wait until options expiration in January to see where the stock is. By then, the stock could be at $96, in which case the put expires worthless.

However, you have to be ready to buy the stock at anytime because the put buyer could make you buy the stock before expiration if she chooses. If put sellers have to buy the underlying stock, it usually doesn't happen until expiration, but it can at any time.

Get the Green Light from Your Broker

To sell covered calls and naked puts, you have to be approved by your broker.

You fill out a form, usually on your broker's website, detailing your options experience, goals, and other information.

There are four levels that you can be approved for.

- Level 1 – Covered calls and long protective puts: This means you can sell covered calls or buy protective puts on stocks you own. It's not difficult to get approved for level 1.
- Level 2 – Long calls and puts: You can speculate by buying calls or puts on stocks you don't own. This level is also not too difficult to get approved.
- Level 3 – Spreads: This is when you buy or sell different strike prices or expiration dates as part of the same trade. Brokers want to know that you're experienced before approval.
- Level 4 – Selling naked calls and puts: Because this has the most risk, it is the most difficult (though not *that* difficult) to get approved for. You'll need to tell the broker that you have experience trading options.

If you can't get approved for Level 4 right away, sell covered calls for a year and then go back to the broker and ask for approval. You'll have more options experience and if you're trading often, they'll see that you're generating commissions, which of course is what they're after.

If you do have a few years of experience with options, it shouldn't be hard to get approved for Level 4 to sell naked puts.

Options have earned a bad reputation because speculators lose money gambling on a stock going up or down. The people who really make money by trading options are the sellers, not the buyers.

Selling covered calls and naked puts is a conservative strategy that can generate hundreds or even thousands of dollars in income per month.

It's a strategy that belongs in your income arsenal.

Actions to Take

- Sell covered calls to generate income on stocks you're okay with selling.
- Never sell naked calls.
- Sell naked puts to generate income on stocks you want to own at a lower price.
- Don't drop your boxers and trade naked in your den. No one wants to see that.

CHAPTER 3

Be the Bank

"Neither a borrower nor lender be."

– Polonius, *Hamlet*

Clearly, Polonius didn't live in as low an interest rate environment as we're in now.

If you need money, you'd be crazy not to borrow it these days.

I'm not a fan of debt, but when the bank is offering 30-year mortgages at lower rates than I can get on a quality dividend paying stock, I'll gladly take the bank's money.

And if you need income, the temptation to lend money at decent yields is strong.

But you don't have to adopt a nickname like Paulie "the Chin" and work out of the back corner of a bar to "put money on the street." Today, there are plenty of ways to lend your money at attractive rates of interest that won't require you to break anyone's thumbs.

Peer-to-Peer Lending

I'm not talking about lending money to your no-good brother-in-law and hoping to get it back. There's a way you can lend to other people's brother-in-laws, with a very real chance of getting your money back. And best of all, you get a decent rate of interest.

Peer-to-peer lending is a way for borrowers, who can't get a loan from a bank, to borrow money from regular folks or other financial institutions, who are willing to lend it to them for a higher rate than they can probably get from a junk bond. And usually with shorter maturities.

But keep in mind, higher rates mean higher risk and peer-to-peer lending definitely has risk.

In a moment, I'll walk you through the details on how to generate 6% to 11% returns. But first, let's understand exactly what peer-to-peer lending is.

If someone needs to consolidate their credit cards, buy a car, or expand a business, but can't get a loan from the bank, they can go to a peer-to-peer lending site like Lending Club (www.lendingclub .com) or Prosper (www.prosper.com). Then, the company creates a "note" for them that will be presented to investors who can choose to "invest" or lend as little as $25.

Once enough people lend the amount that is being asked for, the loan is considered funded. For example, a borrower might request $10,000 and be funded by 250 investors lending $25 to $200 each. After that, the borrower will make fixed monthly payments to repay the loan. Maturities are usually three or five years.

Investors can see a profile of the borrower to help decide whether or not to invest in a note. Though you won't see personal details, you will know the borrower's approximate credit score, income (both within ranges), number of credit lines open, and other details. They will also tell you generally what the money is for, such as debt consolidation, a large purchase, and so on.

A number of years ago, you'd get the person's whole story – something like ...

"I own a small auto repair shop. The competitor down the road just went out of business, and I need $15,000 to expand ..."

Today, you don't get that level of detail. You'll just know it's for a business expansion.

The peer-to-peer lending sites grade the borrowers on a number of factors including credit score. The lower the grade, the higher the interest rate, and you're compensated for taking on higher risk.

It's important to make a lot of loans, even if they're all small, so that a default doesn't ruin your portfolio.

If you have a $1,000 portfolio and you make four loans of $250 each at 6% interest, one default destroys your results.

But if you have 40 loans at $25 each and one of them defaults, you'll still be in the black.

And there will be defaults. That's important to remember.

At Lending Club, the default rates are between 1% and more than 10%[1] depending on the grade of the loan. Interest rates range from 6.7% to 22.8%. Now, 22.8% sounds fantastic, but keep in mind that 10.6% of those loans default.

If you make enough of those very high interest loans and the historical averages continue, you'll make a very nice 12.2%. But you may have to deal with a lot of heartache watching more than a few of those loans go belly up.

If a borrower is late, the site that you're working with (Lending Club, Prosper, etc.) will begin the collections process. They will usually try to contact the borrower to get them back on track. If that doesn't work, they will hand off the process to a collection agency.

If a borrower declares bankruptcy, the company or collections agency are prohibited from contacting them again. If fraud is suspected, the company may sue.

But the reality is: If one of your borrowers stops paying for a few months, the note will probably be written off, and you won't get paid anymore on that loan.

The safest loans on Lending Club, rated A, only have a default rate of 1.3%. They carry a 6.7% average interest rate for a net return of 5.5%, which isn't bad at all today.

But again, be sure to diversify across a large number of loans so that no individual loan hurts your returns too badly.

At Prosper, the estimated default rates range from 1% for the safest loans to more than 17% for the riskiest. Interest rates are between 6.7% and a whopping 31.4% with estimated returns between 4.2% and 11.1%.[2]

Keep in mind: Your net return will not be the same as the interest rate that the borrower is paying because there are fees involved. So the borrower might pay 6%, but because of a 1% fee, you'll get 5%.

Peer-to-peer lending is big business.

Lending Club is a publicly traded company that generated $495 million in operating revenue in 2016 and $8.7 billion in loans.[3] Prosper's revenue was more than $200 million on $3.7 billion

---

[1] http://www.investmentzen.com/peer-to-peer-lending-for-investors/lendingclub.

[2] https://www.prosper.com/about-us/wp-content/uploads/Performance_Update_August.pdf.

[3] http://ir.lendingclub.com/Cache/38285714.pdf?IID=4213397&FID=38285714&O=3&OSID=9.

in loans in 2015. (The company has not released full year 2016 numbers.)[4]

My Experience

I currently have a portfolio with Prosper. All 26 loans are current, though two were late this month. Fortunately, the borrowers made good. Most of my loans are very high quality, rated A or AA, but I do have a few in the riskiest category to try to juice my returns.

My loans are earning between 5.3% and 30.5%. As of today, my annualized yield is 12.1%, though I'm expecting it to go a little lower due to defaults.

As I mentioned, defaults happen, so you want to be diversified. Just like a stock portfolio where you never want one poorly performing stock to sink your nest egg, you don't want one or two bad loans to destroy the good work the rest of the portfolio is doing.

In 2012, Prosper changed the way it assesses the risk of a borrower's defaulting. Since then, defaults have come way down.

In 2013, the default rate across all loan grades combined has ranged between 5.7% and 6.3%.[5] The investor's rate of return (net of defaults) has been between 6.3% and 8.5%.

Now going through the hundreds of available loans might be fun for some. Others just want to put their money to work according to certain parameters. They don't care that the person who is borrowing the money lives in Georgia or is using the money to pay down credit cards.

Investors in the second group can automatically have their funds invested in notes that meet their requirements for the borrower's rating and other criteria. When payments are received and there is enough cash in the account to fund another note, that money can also be automatically reinvested in another loan.

Other peer-to-peer lenders include:

Funding Circle – www.fundingcircle.com provides small business loans from $25,000 to $500,000. You must be an accredited investor (individuals who make $200,000 or more per year for three years in a row, make $300,000 per year jointly for three years in a row, or have $1 million in investable assets not including home equity) to lend

---

[4]https://techcrunch.com/2016/01/30/the-state-of-p2p-lending.
[5]Ibid.

money. Minimum account investment is $50,000, and minimum loan size is $500.

Upstart Investing – www.upstart.com claims to go beyond FICO scores and examine things like academic achievements and work history. Investors must be accredited. The minimum investment amount is $100.

GroundFloor – www.groundfloor.us offers real estate loans with no minimum or maximum amount, but prefers investments of $20,000 to $500,000.[6] It's only available in eight states including California, Texas, and Illinois.[7] GroundFloor plans to expand into others in the near future.

For those who don't care about who they are lending to and are willing to pay for the convenience of having someone else evaluate the loans, there are platforms like **NSRinvest** (www.NSRinvest.com). These companies typically charge 0.6 basis points (0.6%) to manage your portfolio for you and select the loans based on your risk parameters.

NSR's historical returns range from 7.2% for its conservative strategy to 10.7% for its most aggressive strategy.[8]

You can start with any amount of money, though NSR suggests $10,000 to have a well-diversified portfolio.

Streetshares – www.streetshares.com focuses on lending to veteran owned businesses. Investors can fund loans with a minimum of $25 each. These are business loans to veterans to help them expand their businesses. These loans carry a fixed annual interest rate of 5% (subject to change with new loans) and carry one-year terms.

For accredited investors, high-yield investments are available.

These loans can earn an interest rate from 7.9% up to 29.9%, depending on the creditworthiness of the borrower.

Moms and Pops aren't the only ones searching for yield. Big financial institutions like hedge funds are as well and invest in notes on the peer-to-peer sites.

To compete against the big boys, automated services like **LendingRobot** (www.lendingrobot.com) have sprung up to help

---

[6]http://support.groundfloor.us/customer/en/portal/articles/1444213-how-much-money-can-i-borrow-with-groundfloor.

[7]http://support.groundfloor.us/customer/en/portal/articles/1755981-do-i-have-to-be-an-accredited-investor-to-invest-with-groundfloor.

[8]https://www.nsrinvest.com/#user_divide.

individual investors nab the most attractive loans as soon as they become available – before they're snatched up by the institutions.

LendingRobot will handle your peer-to-peer investments for free up to the first $5,000. Then it charges 0.45% on accounts larger than $5,000.

The company claims its algorithms will help peer-to-peer investors lower their risk and improve their returns because it can analyze a loan better than a person can. Perhaps just as importantly, it can do it faster than an individual. And since the best loans often get funded just minutes after they appear on the site, that can be an advantage.

LendingRobot can also help you sell your loans if you want to cash out before they're repaid, or buy loans on the secondary market, though you need $20,000 managed by LendingRobot to take advantage of those services.[9]

I'm currently using LendingRobot with a small amount of money as an experiment to see if the portfolio performs better than what I can do on my own.

Peer-to-peer lending can help generate a solid stream of income, as long as you can handle the ups and downs of late payments and potential defaults.

Family Loans

If the idea of lending your money to a bunch of strangers doesn't sit right or you'd rather lend it to your no good brother-in-law, there are ways you can lend him the money but make it a legal obligation. That way, you're not hounding him at every holiday.

Well, you may still have to ask him for your money, but now you'll have a legal note that can be enforced.

What you need is a promissory note. The note will state the terms (amount, length of the loan, interest rate) that the two of you agree upon. You can find forms on the internet or visit Loanback (www.loanback.com), which helps you create notes, calculate payments, including late fees, and track your loans.

It's a good idea to have the contract notarized, just to give it greater legal standing if your family member defaults.

---

[9]http://docs.lendingrobot.com/article/show/13515-how-do-i-start-trading-on-the-secondary-market.

You must charge interest. This is important.

To avoid it being considered a gift by the Internal Revenue Service, the borrower must pay interest and it has to be a rate that the IRS considers reasonable.

The rate is called the Applicable Federal Rate (AFR) and can change on a monthly basis. You can find the AFR rates at https://apps.irs.gov/app/picklist/list/federalRates.html.

The good news is you're allowed to give your family member a break. As I write this, a short-term loan must carry an interest rate of at least $0.66%, a mid-term loan must be 1.29%, and a long-term loan has to have a minimum rate of 1.95%.[10]

So if you are lending money, not for the income but to help out a relative buy a house, you can charge them as little as 1.95% (be sure to check the AFR when you're making the loan).

I thought I caught a break obtaining a mortgage in the low threes. But if someone had lent me the cash at 1.95%, I'd be beyond thrilled.

You can give money to family members or even loan it to them without interest as long as it's less than $14,000.[11] For anything above $14,000, the IRS wants a piece of it. If your relative is coming to you for cash, the last thing they probably need is to then have to pay a gift tax. They're better off paying you interest on the loan – even if you don't want or need it.

If you are looking for income, there is nothing wrong with charging a reasonable interest rate to your family member. You're not a charity after all – and if you weren't lending the cash to them, you'd have it working for you and generating income. And they would be borrowing the funds at a much higher rate.

For the sake of family relations, I wouldn't charge payday loan or credit card interest rates, but if your relative is looking to consolidate their credit card loans that have 16% interest rates and you charge them 6%, they get a huge reduction in their monthly interest expense and you get a decent rate of return.

Additionally, the terms of the note should spell out exactly what happens if you pass away. Is the note payable immediately? Does the note continue paying into the estate and are the proceeds shared by

---

[10]https://www.irs.gov/pub/irs-drop/rr-16-25.pdf?_ga=1.189575083.1266066666.1431525228.

[11]https://www.irs.gov/businesses/small-businesses-self-employed/frequently-asked-questions-on-gift-taxes.

the heirs? The promissory note is like any other asset in your estate. Make sure you are clear what happens to it if you die.

I've heard of circumstances where an adult grandchild had a rock solid contract with his grandfather on a family loan. When the grandfather died, his kids (the borrower's aunts and uncles) demanded repayment.

Because the grandchild had everything in writing and notarized, the greedy aunts and uncles will have to be content with getting a small payment every month while the loan is paid off.

Also, think about the non-financial aspect of lending money to family. Will this affect your relationship with the family member? With brothers and sisters? Parents, kids, and so on?

While a 6% rate might be enticing in this low-rate environment, it may not be worth the dirty looks across the Thanksgiving dinner table from your sister and brother-in-law because you're demanding that they stick to the $200 per month payment that is outlined in the contract.

But if you trust your relative to keep it professional (and to pay you back), then a family loan can be an excellent way to generate some income while helping out someone you love.

When done right, it can be a win – for everyone.

Go Hard

Hard money lending is a financing method where the loan is backed by an asset - usually real estate. These loans are often bridge loans, carry a high interest rate, and are short term.

An example might be a small homebuilder who is unable to secure financing to finish the home that is being built. The home is either already under contract or will be sold upon completion.

The homebuilder might be too extended to qualify for a bank loan, so he has to find alternative financing. Because he knows he will be paid for the house once it is built, he only needs the money for a year. Since he can't get a loan from the bank, he has to pay a higher interest rate.

The homebuilder finds a group of investors willing to lend him the cash for one year at a 12% interest rate. If he defaults, the investors foreclose on the property. Now, it might be a shell of a house, which they will then have to pay to finish and then sell, or they can sell the incomplete project.

Because the risk is higher than many other types of investments, the interest rate the investor receives is typically higher.

Remember, the loan is backed by real estate, so if things go bad, the investor can foreclose on the real estate, which they can sell to possibly make a profit. Of course, the risk is that the property is no longer (or never was) worth as much as the loan. So investors should carefully assess the value of the asset that is backing the loan.

Hard money lenders also lend to borrowers trying to avoid foreclosure, borrowers refinancing to take cash out but can't verify their income, or a loan where the real estate can't be properly appraised.

Hard money financing is also used by house flippers. Someone who wants to buy a house quickly, then fix it and flip it, may not want to deal with the hassle of applying for a traditional mortgage if they're going to sell the house in less than a year. In that case, it might be worth paying a higher interest rate for six or nine months rather than deal with the red tape and closing costs that come with borrowing from a bank.

The difficult part is finding a borrower. As you can imagine, in this low interest rate environment, investors are desperately searching for yield and willing to take on higher degrees of risk for less and less yield.

So it's competitive.

It helps to know someone that has put together these types of loans before. Preferably, someone who is familiar with the market where the real estate is located, so that they can determine whether the real estate is worth the amount of the loan and the likelihood of the asset maintaining its value if the borrower defaults. The investor should also have a game plan for exiting the investment if the borrower defaults and they foreclose on the property.

Keep in mind, this is speculative stuff. A borrower who defaults won't just come by your house and hand you the keys. The property could be tied up in the courts for a long time. Meanwhile, you don't have access to your principal and it is no longer generating any income.

But if you can handle the risk, hard money lending can earn you double-digit yields.

How Do You Get Started?

You can of course search the internet for companies or brokers that put borrowers and lenders together. However, I recommend only working with someone who you know personally or was referred to you by someone you trust.

There are too many scammers out there, and the amounts of money needed to participate is usually large. I've never seen terms for less than $25,000 per investor. And it's usually higher.

So you want to know who you're doing business with.

If you know any realtors in your area, they may be able to put you in touch with a broker or someone who puts these deals together. You definitely want a referral.

Hard money loans are unregistered securities so if the deal goes bad and you lose money, you can't go complaining to the Securities and Exchange Commission. I mean, technically you could, but it's not going to do anything about it.

The only recourse you'd have is to prove fraud and sue on those grounds. But if there was no fraud committed and the investment just didn't turn out the way you expected (remember some of these borrowers aren't creditworthy according to banks), then you're simply out of luck.

Crowdfunding

There are crowdfunding sites like RealtyShares (www.realtyshares .com), where investors can invest in real estate equity or debt by buying a share of a property or owning a piece of the debt. The investor chooses which option she prefers.

Peer Street (www.peerstreet.com) is a service where investors can invest in debt only. Peer Street manages the servicing of the loans, including foreclosure if necessary, for a fee that ranges from 0.25% to 1.0%.

These types of platforms offer investors a choice of which specific loans or properties to invest in. If you only want to invest in single-family homes on the West Coast that will yield 10%, you can wait for that investment to be offered. Or in some cases, you can set parameters and have your money automatically invested.

You must be an accredited investor to use these sites. Again, that means you have to make $200,000 per year or $300,000 jointly per year for three years in a row or have a net worth of $1 million. But you don't have to invest big money into each investment. Many of the various platforms have minimum investments of $1,000. That's significantly less than the $25,000 to $50,000 minimums you usually see with privately arranged deals.

Investing with the crowdfunding sites isn't exactly like investing in hard money financing. Some terms may be the same, such as the fact that the debt is backed by the real estate, but the interest rate will usually be lower.

Crowdfunding real estate has only been around since about 2013, so it's too early to determine if the risk is higher or lower by investing through those types of sites – particularly because the market has gone straight up since 2013.

With crowdfunding, you pay a management fee and the crowd-funding company supposedly vets the borrower and property.

However, like I explained before, these are risky investments. I don't trust anyone who I don't know personally or haven't been referred to by someone I know.

Just like I would never invest with a stockbroker I don't know, I'm not about to invest in real estate through a nameless, faceless company.

But if you feel differently, those sites are worth exploring.

First Position Commercial Mortgages

Another way to invest in private real estate loans is through First Position Commercial Mortgages (FPCM).

These are similar to hard money loans with one glaring difference: When you invest in an FPCM you are lending your money to the FPCM company, not the borrower. The FPCM company then lends the money to the borrower – typically someone who would look for a hard money loan.

That little detail matters for two important reasons:

1. You'll collect lower interest on your loan.
2. Your loan is "guaranteed" by the FPCM company.

The FPCM company takes your money, pays you a rate of interest, and lends it out at a higher interest rate.

Typically, if you lend cash to a hard money borrower, you will get a 10% to 12% interest rate. With an FPCM, the FPCM company will lend at 10% to 12% and pay you 5% to 6%.

What do you get for that 5% to 6% that the FPCM company is paying?

They find the loan, which you may not be able to do yourself. However, if you used a third party such as a broker or partner for hard money loans, you would usually pay 1%, not 5% or 6%.

But FPCMs usually "guarantee" you'll receive your monthly payments *even if the borrower stops paying.* For some investors, that may well be worth the 5% to 6% that they're giving up.

I put guarantee in quotes because the FPCM is not necessarily obligated to pay you if the borrower defaults. They say they will, but they don't have to.

The industry is brand spankin' new. It's only been around since 2012. Since then, there don't appear to be many instances of FPCMs defaulting on their payments to investors.

That being said, it's easy to log an impressive track record in a raging bull market for real estate.

If a borrower defaults, the FPCM company can continue to pay investors, knowing that it will sell the property for more than the loan is worth – both because of the low loan-to-value ratio and because real estate prices have been rising.

I'd like to see the track records after the next recession or slump in real estate. If they continue to make investors whole after borrower defaults, then I may consider them a worthy investment.

But for now, they are too young and unproven. And you're only earning 5% or 6% to lend money to a borrower that the market has determined should pay 10% to 12%. In other words, you're taking a big risk but only getting a medium payout.

If after the next downturn the FPCMs have proven that the risk is in fact not large, then 5% or 6% may be reasonable. But until they can prove the business model while real estate prices are falling, they are not worth the risk.

Whether you're a bank, a loan shark, or a participant in the peer-to-peer sites, lending money for interest has been a way to earn income for hundreds of years. Today, there are various ways you can participate and generate some strong yields if you're willing to accept the risk.

Actions to Take

- Check out peer-to-peer lending if you want someone else to assess the borrower's risk and keep track of all the paperwork.
- If you're lending to family or friends, get a signed, notarized legal document that spells out all of the terms.
- If you're interested in hard money deals, only work with someone you know and trust.
- If you want to call yourself Paulie "the Chin," go ahead. You can pull it off.

Become the IRS: Have People Pay Taxes to You

"The tax code is a monstrosity and there's only one thing to do with it. Scrap it, kill it, drive a stake through its heart, bury it and hope it never rises again to terrorize the American people."

– Steve Forbes

Unfortunately, Steve Forbes' statement is a pipe dream. The U.S. tax code isn't going anywhere anytime soon. So in the spirit of "if you can't beat 'em, join 'em," this chapter shows you how you can become the near equivalent of the Internal Revenue Service.

Imagine if you had the taxing authority of the IRS, or your state, or local government. That would take care of your retirement needs in a jiffy.

Surprisingly, there is a way for you to collect taxes from your fellow citizens. And you won't have to pave their roads or collect their garbage to do so.

When you purchase tax lien certificates, *you* receive the tax payments from an individual taxpayer rather than the government.

Here's how it works:

A homeowner falls behind on his real estate taxes. Rather than foreclosing on the home and auctioning it off, the county auctions off the tax bill. The buyer who accepts the lowest interest rate on the tax bill wins.

So if a homeowner owes $5,000, the county auctions off the $5,000 bill. Anyone who bids is offering to pay the county $5,000. One buyer may start the bidding at 12% interest. The next brings it down to 11% and so on. Perhaps at the end, the winning bid is 5%, though some states have different rules on how much an investor can earn (more on that later).

The winner pays the county $5,000 (plus whatever fees are required to participate in the bidding process). The buyer is now owed $5,000 from the homeowner, plus the annual interest.

Tax lien certificates typically earn 4% to 7% per year.[1] What's nice about this type of program is that the investment is backed by property that is typically worth much more than the amount of money you shelled out.

You're essentially making a loan (often a small one) on behalf of the homeowner, and the home is the collateral.

If the homeowner fails to pay the $5,000-plus interest, at a certain point the owner of the tax lien certificate can foreclose. So it's possible for a buyer of tax lien certificates to wind up with a property for just the $5,000 tax bill (plus expenses related to the foreclosure).

Now, if they have any equity in the house, most homeowners will find a way to come up with the $5,000, or whatever they owe, to avoid losing their home.

Only 0.5% of tax lien certificates are foreclosed before they are redeemed.[2] So don't buy tax lien certificates because you think you're going to get a property dirt cheap. You probably won't. You should buy tax lien certificates because you can get an attractive interest rate. If you wind up with the property, that's a bonus.

You can increase your odds of owning the home by only buying certificates where there is no mortgage on the property. If a bank still holds a mortgage, it will probably pay the tax itself, rather than let the county take the property and sell it.

Some states like Florida do not grant the holder of the tax lien certificate an automatic deed to the property if the homeowner does not pay the tax bill. In Florida's case, after two years the property is auctioned. The certificate owner is allowed to participate in the auction process but is not guaranteed to end up with the property.

Should someone else win the property, the certificate owner will get paid what he or she is owed plus interest.

---

[1]http://www.forbes.com/sites/morganbrennan/2012/11/26/vulture-investing-what-you-need-to-know-before-bidding-for-tax-liens/#5fdb5b70345e.

[2]http://www.cnbc.com/2017/01/27/heres-why-you-could-have-property-tax-liens-in-your-portfolio.html.

How and Where to Buy Tax Lien Certificates

Roughly half of the counties in the United States use tax lien certificates to collect unpaid taxes. The remaining half simply foreclose on the properties and auction them off.

As mentioned earlier, each state and county has different rules and may have maximum and minimum returns that buyers can earn.

For example, in Florida, the minimum you will earn as an investor is 5%, while the maximum is 18%. The property owner has two years to pay the taxes and interest. You can earn a maximum of 16% in Arizona, and the taxpayer can take three years to pay.

Tax liens are usually sold once a year. Check with the county's tax collector's office for the date of the auction and procedures. You often have to register ahead of time.

In most cases, you don't have to be local or present at the auction to buy a tax lien certificate. You can bid online or in the mail.

Since rules are different for every county and state, be sure to understand the process for any county and state that you are interested in.

Most counties have the list of available certificates online. Take a look at the ones that interest you. You'll want to do some research to make sure there are no other liens on the property that are ahead of you. Usually a tax lien is first in line, but you don't want any surprises.

If you win an auction and buy a tax lien certificate, you want to register it with the County Clerk's office right away. That way, if the owner sells the property, you'll show up as a lien holder and will be first in line to get paid.

When the homeowner pays his taxes, he will pay it to the county, not to you. The county will then send you the money.

Keep in mind, you and I are not the only people who know about tax lien certificates. There are professional investors, even hedge funds, that specialize in tax lien certificates. So they often buy up the most attractive tax liens at low interest rates.

Go Over-the-Counter

There is another way you can buy tax lien certificates without participating in the auction process. Like the mousy wallflower who doesn't get asked to dance, there are often tax liens that are neglected by other investors. Many times there is a valid reason. The owner may be in bankruptcy proceedings (see "Due Diligence" section), or there may be other issues.

But for investors who enjoy digging for values, over-the-counter (OTC) tax lien certificates may be the way to go.

An OTC tax lien is a lien that wasn't sold via the traditional auction method. It is leftover. As a result, anyone who buys the OTC certificate will receive the highest allowable interest rate.

Remember, in the auction process, buyers bid down the interest rate. The winner is the person who will accept the lowest rate.

With an OTC tax lien certificate, there is no bidding. No one wants it except you. So you are awarded the top interest rate, which can be well into the double digits.

Some counties have a standard process in place for offering OTC certificates. Others don't have a process and you may even come across county employees who have no idea what you're talking about.

If the county doesn't publish the available OTC certificates, you may have to speak to the County Tax Collector directly and ask that a list be sent to you and to find out what steps you need to take to buy an OTC tax lien certificate.

The good news is you probably won't have much competition; however, OTC tax lien certificates are becoming more popular, so you'll want to act quickly after the initial tax lien auction.

Once you own the OTC tax lien certificate, the process is the same as if you'd bought it at auction.

You will be notified if the tax lien was paid, though it's not a bad idea to check with the Tax Collector's office every so often to make sure nothing slipped through the cracks.

If the time limit expires, you will be notified that you must file for the deed or that the property will be auctioned off.

But stay on top of it. We know that government offices are overworked and understaffed. It's your money, so be sure you know the dates that everything is supposed to happen and call the Tax Collector's office if those dates pass without receiving any notice or payments.

Due Diligence

The last thing you want is a big headache when it comes to your investments. You probably don't have the desire or the time to deal with lawyers and government bureaucrats trying to sort out a legal web in regards to your tax lien certificates.

The following guidelines may help you stay out of trouble. It will take a little digging, but it will be well worth your time.

Avoid properties:

- If the County Tax Collector and Property Appraiser's records are not in agreement. For example, if one shows that the building you're interested in is a two-bedroom house and the other says it's a three-bedroom house, or the square footage is different, or any other inconsistency.
- If there are other claims to title on the property besides for the listed taxpayer.
- If there is a bankruptcy involved: Your money could be tied up for years until the bankruptcy is settled, and it's possible you won't get your money back.
- If there are other tax liens.

Avoiding these issues will minimize unnecessary complications. There are plenty of tax lien certificates available without any of those issues.

You may also want to drive by the properties you are interested in – if you can. Just so you can see that they truly exist and that if the tax collector says there's a house on it, that there is in fact a house on it.

Do not contact the owner of the property. Many states explicitly forbid you from doing so, even after you've bought the tax lien certificate.

Drive by, take a look, and move on.

Tax lien certificates are an easy concept to understand. You're essentially paying someone's taxes for them. In return, they owe you the money, plus interest. If they don't pay you back, in many states you have the right to foreclose on their property.

However, the rules can be complex. So be sure you understand each state's and county's laws regarding tax lien certificates before investing. The information is usually available on the County Tax Collector's website.

Once you have a firm grasp of how it works, tax lien certificates can be a great way to earn a solid interest rate and maybe even an extremely high one – backed by real estate that is worth many times your investment.

This is a particularly attractive strategy for retirees who may have the time to devote to understanding the rules and hunting for a bargain.

Actions to Take

- Thoroughly understand the rules of your state and county before investing in tax lien certificates.
- Consider OTC tax lien certificates if you don't win an auction or don't want to participate in one.
- Do your due diligence on the property you're interested in to avoid headaches.
- Just because someone owes you tax money doesn't make you the IRS. If you try to audit someone, it won't go well.

5

Get Paid More from Social Security

"We can never insure one hundred percent of the population against one hundred percent of the hazards and vicissitudes of life, but we have tried to frame a law which will give some measure of protection to the average citizen and to his family against the loss of a job and against poverty-ridden old age."

– President Franklin Delano Roosevelt upon signing the
Social Security Act

There's nothing like the Federal government to take a good idea and complicate it to the point of maximum frustration.

On August 14, 1935, President Franklin Delano Roosevelt signed the Social Security Act to help the nation's elderly pay for some of life's basics.[1]

Prior to 1934, more than half of elderly Americans did not have sufficient income to support themselves.[2]

Today, the numbers aren't much better. Forty-five percent of Americans over the age of 65 have annual incomes of $23,500 or less.[3]

But the big difference is most seniors today can rely on at least some income from Social Security.

---

[1] https://www.ssa.gov/history/briefhistory3.html.

[2] Ibid.

[3] http://kff.org/medicare/issue-brief/poverty-among-seniors-an-updated-analysis-of-national-and-state-level-poverty-rates-under-the-official-and-supplemental-poverty-measures.

It's not much. The average monthly benefit is $1,248,[4] which comes out to $14,976 per year. But it's better than nothing, particularly if you have no savings or other source of income.

However, we don't settle for average.

This chapter explores various ways to maximize your social security benefits. You paid into the system for 30 or 40 years. You're entitled to every dollar you can legally squeeze out of it.

But the government sure doesn't make it easy for you to do that. And why would they? Beginning in 2020, Social Security will pay out more than it takes in. Unless something changes, there will be nothing left in the kitty by 2034[5] (just when I'm about to start collecting – terrific).

To make it difficult for you to figure out just how much you can collect, the Social Security agency created a handbook that is 27 chapters long.[6]

Each chapter is broken into sections. Most chapters have 25 to 40 sections. The shortest, on black lung benefits, has just one section. If you want to read about supplemental income benefits, you'll want to go to Chapter 21 and it's 97 sections.

If you don't want to read 27 chapters of the Social Security Handbook, you can just visit a Social Security office or call it on the phone and get the help you need right away.

I'll wait until you stop laughing.

Huge cuts in staff and office closures have made it difficult to get help from a person.

A 2014 survey found 14% of callers get busy signals. If you do get through, it is common to wait for 20 minutes or longer. If you visit an office, bring something to read. Maybe pack a lunch. You can expect to wait at least two hours.[7]

It's almost as if they're trying to make the Department of Motor Vehicles look good.

And it's not because the representatives are lazy and unwilling to help you. They are swamped. Between 2010 and 2014, 64 offices

---

[4]https://www.ssa.gov/policy/docs/quickfacts/stat_snapshot.

[5]https://www.ssa.gov/oact/trsum.

[6]https://www.ssa.gov/OP_Home/handbook/handbook-toc.html.

[7]https://www.wsj.com/articles/calling-social-security-expect-a-wait-1404000761.

closed, and 533 mobile offices were shuttered. Before the cuts, 90% of applicants could schedule an appointment within three weeks. By 2015, fewer than half could.[8]

Now that you're frustrated just thinking about trying to get some help, let's cut through the wait times and help you maximize your benefits.

First, a few basic rules:

The full retirement age is 65, if you're born before 1943. The full retirement age is the minimum age you can collect your full benefits. You can start collecting as early as age 62, but the benefits will be reduced by 25%. So in most cases you're better off waiting until the full retirement age or later (I'll explain) to get the most money.

If you were born between 1943 and 1954, the full retirement age is 66. It climbs toward 67 if you came into this world between 1955 and 1959. Anyone who was born in 1960 or later has to wait until age 67 for full retirement benefits.

You can also delay when you begin collecting until age 70. If you do, you get an additional 8% per year that you waited, once the checks start rolling in.

Considering average life expectancy is 84.3 years for a 65-year-old man and 86.6 for a 65-year-old woman, you're usually better off waiting until 70 to collect.

Let's say you're 67 years old and can start collecting the average $1,248 per month or $14,976 per year. If you live to 84.3 years, you'll collect $274,060.

However, if you put off taking your benefits until age 70 – because of the extra 8% per year that you delayed (32% total) – you'll earn $302,450.

Your annual benefit is $19,768 instead of $14,976.

You can see how the numbers play out in three scenarios – taking benefits early at age 62, taking them at full retirement at 67, and waiting until age 70. We assume the retiree is earning the average annual benefit (plus or minus penalties or additional benefits for early or deferred retirement age) and an average lifespan of 84.3 years.

---

[8]http://www.cbpp.org/research/retirement-security/budget-cuts-squeeze-social-security-administration-even-as-workloads.

Early retirement age 62	Annual Social Security income	Full retirement age 67	Annual Social Security income	Deferred retirement age 70	Annual Social Security income
62	$11,232	62	$0	62	$0
63	$11,232	63	$0	63	$0
64	$11,232	64	$0	64	$0
65	$11,232	65	$0	65	$0
66	$11,232	66	$0	66	$0
67	$11,232	67	$14,976	67	$0
68	$11,232	68	$14,976	68	$0
69	$11,232	69	$14,976	69	$0
70	$11,232	70	$14,976	70	$19,768
71	$11,232	71	$14,976	71	$19,768
72	$11,232	72	$14,976	72	$19,768
73	$11,232	73	$14,976	73	$19,768
74	$11,232	74	$14,976	74	$19,768
75	$11,232	75	$14,976	75	$19,768
76	$11,232	76	$14,976	76	$19,768
77	$11,232	77	$14,976	77	$19,768
78	$11,232	78	$14,976	78	$19,768
79	$11,232	79	$14,976	79	$19,768
80	$11,232	80	$14,976	80	$19,768
81	$11,232	81	$14,976	81	$19,768
82	$11,232	82	$14,976	82	$19,768
83	$11,232	83	$14,976	83	$19,768
84	$11,232	84	$14,976	84	$19,768
84.3	$3,369	84.3	$4,492	84.3	$5,930
Total Social Security income	$250,473	Total Social Security income	$274,060	Total Social Security income	$302,450

You can see what a huge difference it makes to defer collecting benefits as long as you can.

Even though someone receiving benefits at 62 years old collects income for eight more years than another who defers until 70 years old, the latter will collect nearly $52,000 more over the course of his lifetime (assuming they both live to the average age).

The person who starts collecting at 70 receives over $28,000 more than the one who collects at the full retirement age of 67.

Based on life expectancies, the spread is even wider for women since they live an average of 2.3 years longer than men.

Keep in mind, these figures don't include the cost of living allowance (COLA) increase, which varies each year. With inflation low for the past decade, the COLA increase has been puny.

In 2017, Social Security recipients got a whopping increase of 0.3%. So on an average $14,976 annual benefit, retirees received an additional $44.92, or $3.74 a month.

If you claim benefits at full retirement age and then change your mind, you can withdraw your application in the first 12 months, pay back the money and then earn the delay credits. If you took early retirement benefits at 62, you don't have to pay it back; just stop the benefits at retirement age (65) and earn the delay credits.[9]

How Much Will You Get?

Social Security is designed to replace 40% of income for most Americans.

The amount you will receive is based on your 35 highest years of earning income. If there are any years when you didn't earn income, zeroes will be included in the average.

For example, if you earn $50,000 every year for 35 years, your Social Security will be based on an average annual income of $50,000. But if you did not work for three of those years, your average comes down to $45,714. That could mean the difference between a $1,397 monthly benefit and $1,322. That $75-per-month difference comes out to $900 per year.

So if you have zero- or low-income years as part of your top 35, consider working longer. Not only will you make the income from work, but it will increase your Social Security benefit.

The maximum benefit in 2017 is $3,538 per month.[10]

Sounds simple, right? Here's where it can get trickier – spousal benefits.

Your spouse can claim 50% of your benefits, once you file. So if your benefit is $2,000, your spouse can collect $1,000.

What if your spouse is already receiving his or her own benefits? They can't double dip so they have to choose which one is larger.

If the 50% rule is larger than your spouse's own benefit, he or she can claim the higher spousal benefit once you start collecting.

---

[9]http://www.kiplinger.com/slideshow/retirement/T051-S001-what-you-must-know-about-social-security/index.html.

[10]http://www.usatoday.com/story/sponsor-story/motley-fool/2016/12/13/whats-maximum-social-security-benefit-2017/95088994.

Know Your Numbers

If you're not yet collecting Social Security, you can check to see how much your estimated payout will be by visiting the Social Security Administration's website at www.ssa.gov/myaccount.

You'll have to create an account on the website and enter your name, birthday, Social Security number, and other private information, so be sure to only do so on a secure network.

There are other quick calculators out there based on how much you're earning now, but because Social Security benefits are built on your earnings history, these quick calculators are next to useless.

If you want an accurate accounting of your likely benefits, take the few minutes to create an account on the Social Security Administration's site.

Additionally, you'll be able to see your earnings history and make any corrections if there's a mistake. Big government agencies have been known to make errors every once in a while.

For example, let's say your spouse is collecting $500 per month. Once you start collecting your own benefit of $2,000 per month, your spouse can claim spousal benefits and receive $1,000 per month instead of the $500 she previously received.[11] Combined, you'd receive $3,000 per month.

Now, here's something that will be a blessing to some people and will drive others nuts. Ex-spouses may be entitled to some spousal benefits. The good news is a person's benefits are not affected by an ex-spouse collecting spousal benefits. And they won't even know about it if they are already divorced.

An ex-spouse is eligible for benefits if:

1. They are at least 62 years old AND
2. They are unmarried AND
3. The marriage lasted 10 years or longer AND
4. Their own benefits are less than what they'd receive from spousal benefits.[12]

---

[11] http://www.kiplinger.com/slideshow/retirement/T051-S001-what-you-must-know-about-social-security/index.html.

[12] http://www.kiplinger.com/article/retirement/T051-C032-S015-a-hidden-social-security-windfall-for-divorcees.html.

They can even claim spousal benefits before the ex takes their own, but they must be divorced for two years.[13] An ex can also continue to work while receiving spousal benefits.[14]

To collect spousal benefits based on an ex-spouse, you must have been married for 10 years or longer and not be remarried. If you are collecting an ex-spousal benefit and get remarried, you will no longer receive those benefits.

So if your new love didn't earn as much as your ex, you may want to hold off on the nuptials. Otherwise, your benefits will decrease.

The ex collecting ex-spousal benefits does not receive the credits for a delayed benefit. So if the ex delays receiving benefits until age 70, the one claiming ex-spousal benefits will only receive 50% of the full retirement age benefit.

In 2016, a very important change was made to spousal benefits. I bring this up because some people may be giving out incorrect advice to retirees.

The previous law allowed a spouse to take spousal benefits while delaying their own – accumulating that extra 8% per year up until age 70. Then at age 70, they would switch to the higher benefit.

That is no longer allowed.

Beginning in January 2016, if a spouse files for spousal benefits, they will automatically be filed for both spousal and their own benefits. It is called a "deemed filing." The applicant will receive the larger of the two payments. So they can no longer earn spousal benefits while accumulating the 8% per year deferral credits.[15]

Survivor Benefits

If your spouse passes away, you are entitled to survivor benefits.

You can claim survivor benefits beginning at:

- Age 50 if you are disabled (benefit will be reduced).
- Age 60 if you are not disabled (benefit will be reduced).

---

[13]http://www.kiplinger.com/slideshow/retirement/T051-S001-what-you-must-know-about-social-security/index.html.

[14]http://www.kiplinger.com/article/retirement/T051-C032-S015-a-hidden-social-security-windfall-for-divorcees.html.

[15]https://www.ssa.gov/planners/retire/claiming.html.

- Full retirement age (you get 100% of deceased spouse's benefit, regardless of whether you previously took a reduced benefit).
- Over the age of 70, you get the higher benefit of yours or your deceased spouse's.

Like most situations regarding Social Security, it usually pays to delay. If your benefit with the extra 32% at age 70 will be higher than your survivor benefit, then it usually makes sense to take the survivor benefit while delaying your own. Then, at age 70, you can take the higher of the two.

Here's an example:

You and your spouse are both full retirement age. Your spouse's benefit is $2,000 per month and yours is $1,800. Your spouse passes away. You can collect the $2,000 per month while delaying your own benefit to earn the extra 8% per year or 32% total credit.

Then at age 70, your $1,800 is now $2,376. So you switch from collecting the survivor benefit to your own.

If you are younger than full retirement age, you'll want to walk through the numbers with an accountant to figure out which strategy makes the most sense for you, It will change depending on the amount your benefit is reduced because you are under the full retirement age.

Children under the age of 18 receive 75% of what the deceased would receive if they were at full retirement.

And if you had children late in life and are collecting Social Security while you have a minor child, they are eligible to receive up to one half your benefit. That's in addition to what you are collecting.

Now, I wouldn't go making babies just to collect an extra $800 or so per month, but, hey, kids are expensive. Every little bit helps. So if you are collecting Social Security and have a child under the age of 18, be sure to collect that money for them. You can put it into a 529 Plan and get a head start on paying for their education.

Taxes

While you're working, Uncle Sam taxes your income and repossesses your money to pay for Social Security; then when he gives it back to you, he taxes it. That's right. You may have to pay taxes on Social Security.

If you earn income more than what you receive in Social Security, there's a good chance you'll have business with the IRS.

Up to 85% of your Social Security payments may be subject to tax if . . .

One-half of the amount of your adjusted gross income, including tax-exempt interest, plus one-half of your Social Security benefits, exceeds:

1. $25,000 if you are single;
2. $25,000 if you are married and not filing a joint return, and you did not live with your spouse at any time during the year;
3. $32,000 if you are married and filing a joint return.[16]

An interesting and important note: Interest from municipal bonds, which is usually tax free, is included in the calculation for adjusted gross income when it comes to figuring out whether you'll pay taxes on Social Security.

A couple of ways to try to lower your adjusted gross income:

1. Withdraw money from tax-free Roth IRAs. Those funds are not included in adjusted gross income.
2. Make charitable donations from your regular IRA or 401k. The donation counts as part of your required minimum distribution, but if the gift is made directly from the retirement account, it does not count towards your adjusted gross income.

One last word on Social Security:

Make sure your numbers are right. The Social Security Administration makes mistakes.

They now send paper statements only every five years. But you can check online anytime at https://www.ssa.gov/myaccount. You set up an account by providing the same personal information I mentioned in the Know Your Numbers box. Make sure you are on a secure network. In other words, don't do it at Starbucks or in a hotel.

You will then be asked some multiple choice questions that will prove you are who you say you are. They may ask which bank you

---

[16]https://www.ssa.gov/OP_Home/handbook/handbook.01/handbook-0125 .html.

have your auto loan with, what type of car you own, a previous phone number, and so on. They know a lot about you. It's creepy.

Once the account is set up, you can view what your expected benefits are and your wage history.

Remember, since your benefits are based on wage history, make sure that every dollar that you earned in the past is included. If Social Security has wrong data on your wages, you can correct it no matter how many years ago it was – as long as you have proof (an old tax return, W-2, etc.).

If the incorrect income was from self-employment, you can only correct it up to three years, three months, and 15 days after the end of the year in which the income was earned.

Social Security is a vital way for most people to pay for necessities in retirement. Be certain you are getting every dollar you're entitled to.

Hopefully, I've just saved you two hours of waiting at the Social Security office.

Actions to Take

- Make sure you understand the various rules that will dictate how much money you will receive.
- If your health is good and you have reason to believe you have plenty of years left, do whatever you can to delay taking benefits until age 70.
- Set up an account at www.ssa.gov/myaccount to ensure that all of your earnings information is correct.
- Read the Social Security handbook if you're having trouble sleeping.

CHAPTER 6

You Don't Have to Drive for Uber – But You May Want To

"Have you ever noticed that anybody driving slower than you is an idiot, and anyone going faster than you is a maniac?"

– George Carlin

I could have easily called this book "You Don't Have to Be a Wal-Mart Greeter in Retirement," but mentioning Uber in the title was better for marketing.

The sentiment is the same. If you read this book, you won't need a part-time job that you don't want in order to live comfortably.

However, some people love the idea of working in retirement, especially if it's part-time.

Uber, Lyft, and other ride-sharing services offer those opportunities. Drivers don't have to be out on the road when they don't want to be. They don't have to drive to places they don't want to. It's total freedom. Of course, the more flexible you are, the more hours you work; and the more you hustle, the more money you'll make.

But the part-timer that wants to drive just a few hours a month to make some extra cash can do exactly that.

What's especially attractive for retirees is that Uber drivers can set their own schedule or no schedule. (I'm going to reference Uber throughout this chapter, but it can be any of the ride-sharing services unless otherwise noted.) Drivers don't have to tell Uber when they'll be on the clock. There are no managers to report to and no shifts that you have to show up for.

If you babysit the grandkids Mondays, have a golf game Tuesdays and Thursdays and dinner plans Wednesday night, you don't have to drive at those times. If your Thursday golf game gets cancelled, you can drive for a few hours that day to pay for next week's greens fees. It's entirely up to you.

If you're unfamiliar with Uber, it's very simple. It's like a taxi, but rather than hailing one on the street or calling a phone number where a dispatcher will send one out, customers have an app on their phone. They enter their location and where they are going. The first driver to accept the request on the app on their own phone gets the job.

Customers rate the drivers from one to five on both Uber and Lyft.

If your ride is fine with no problems, you should give the driver five stars. Even if the service wasn't out of this world. That's because drivers are required to maintain a 4.6 rating.

Obviously, if you had a problem with a driver, rate them accordingly. But five stars is the standard.

This is a great feature of the ridesharing services. When you hail a cab, you have no idea if you're getting a nice guy or some lunatic. I've had plenty of both. And because there is no feedback or accountability, many cab drivers have no incentive for good service (other than a tip).

We've all had the unpleasant cab driver who drives like a maniac, hasn't showered in weeks, or rants like a madman. Unless he does something criminal, that driver will stay on the roads.

With Uber and Lyft, there is accountability and they can be fired.

The flip side of all this is that the drivers also rate the customer. If you're abusive, obnoxious, or display otherwise nasty behavior, you'll be rated low. That's a warning to other drivers not to pick you up.

Don't worry, if you have one bad experience with a driver and he gives you one star, you're not going to be stranded in the rain the next time you need a ride. But give enough drivers grief and your low rating will be a red flag to other drivers.

As a driver, that's another benefit. Not only can you decide when and where you're going to drive (customers enter their pick up and destination information), but also who you're going to drive.

If someone in your neighborhood needs a ride to the airport and you don't feel like driving that far, you ignore the request.

If the pickup and destination are fine, but the rider has a 2.2 rating, you can decide whether you want this person in your car or not.

In other words, there is a ton of flexibility.

How Much Can You Make?

That's the important question, isn't it?

Generally speaking you'll earn about $15 to $20 per hour. If you're in a big city and demand is heavy, you may make as much as $30 per hour.

You can also receive a sign-up bonus of around $500 when you start. Sometimes the companies run special promotions where the bonus is larger. I've seen sign-up bonuses run as high as $1,200.

However, *you'll usually need to be referred by an existing driver.* So if you're seriously considering driving for Uber, the next time you go out to dinner, take an Uber instead of driving so that you understand the experience and get a referral code from a driver.

You can also find referral codes online. Just Google "Uber new driver referral code" or something similar, and you'll have several options.

If you get the bonus, don't think about taking the money and running. It won't work. To get paid the bonus, you usually have to drive between 50 and 100 trips in your first month.

So even though it's as flexible as you want it to be, you do have to put in some time to get a sign-up bonus as a new driver.

How Does It Work?

Uber pays its drivers every week.

Like a taxi, fares are based on the length of the trip and how long the passenger is in the car. There is also a booking fee. Uber collects the booking fee and 25% of the fare.

Each city has different rates. A driver in Los Angeles will probably earn more than one in Abilene, Texas.

Drivers can make more during surge pricing. Surge pricing occurs when there is more demand for rides than supply. Uber charges higher rates depending on how big the demand is. Sometimes rates will be 1.3 times the normal rate. Other times it will be triple.

As a driver, that means more money for you. So if you're serious about making extra cash, you might want to make sure you're on the road during commuting hours and Friday and Saturday nights. If there is a big convention, concert, or sporting event in town, you probably want to be nearby when it's letting out.

Keep in mind that you will only make money when you have a fare in your car. You are not paid for waiting or driving to a customer.

It used to be that Uber drivers did not get tips. Now, the rider can tip through the app. Drivers keep 100% of the tip. Uber does not collect a percentage.

While some passengers may tip with cash, many use the app. It's one of the attractive features from a customer standpoint – no cash has to change hands.

And as far as safety is concerned, the Uber driver isn't a target like a cab driver who is sitting on a wad of cash. Anyone who is familiar with Uber knows that the drivers aren't paid at the time services are rendered, so it's safer than driving a cab.

Of course, any time you're allowing strangers in your car, there is some risk, but generally Uber is safer than a cab from the driver standpoint. Since customers have to register personal information with Uber when they sign up, Uber knows who is getting in your car. You don't, other than the customers' rating, but if anything happens, Uber knows who used the app for that ride.

Requirements

You must be 21 years old with three years of driving experience in the United States or 23 years old with one-year driving experience – not commercial driving, mind you, just driving.

Considering this book is about living comfortably in retirement, I'm guessing the age requirement isn't going to be a deal breaker for anyone reading this.

Uber will do a background check on you.

You will not be allowed to drive for Uber if you have a DUI in the past seven years, were involved in a fatal accident, or have a history of reckless driving or a criminal record.

Your car will need to be a 2001 model year or later, have in-state license plates, and pass an Uber inspection.[1]

---

[1]https://www.dropbox.com/s/udueh5a1y4snf67/Uber%20Driver%20Training%20Guide.pdf?dl=0.

If you need a car to drive for Uber, the company may help you obtain one through its marketplace, short-term leasing service, or with a loan. However, Uber's loans and leasing programs are typically not the best deal in town. And as of August 2017, Uber was talking about closing its leasing program.

That's not necessarily a bad thing for drivers.

To get a lease, drivers pay $250 up front and make weekly payments that are taken right out of their Uber earnings.[2]

The leases are expensive. In a March 2016 article, *Bloomberg* detailed one driver's experience. She had to pay $155 per week. At the end of the three-year lease, she will have paid Uber $25,210 for a 2015 Honda Civic. If she wants to keep the car after the lease, she will have to pay Uber an additional $5,000.

The Kelley Blue Book Value of a 2015 Honda Civic is $18,142.[3]

So if you can find financing or a lease anywhere else, do it. You'll probably get a better deal than you will with Uber.

Insurance

This is perhaps the most misunderstood and vitally important thing to know about driving for Uber.

Your personal auto insurance doesn't cover you while driving for commercial purposes.

If you get into an accident while driving for Uber, you are on your own as far as insurance goes. Your insurer will not cover the damage or liability.

If you're driving for Uber and logged on to the app, Uber will provide some insurance. There are three distinct periods, and the coverage changes depending on which period you're in.

Period 1 – The app is on and you're waiting for a request.

You could be parked on the side of the road or driving around waiting for a fare. The important thing is that you have not accepted a request. During this period, if you get into an accident, Uber *will not* provide any collision insurance. It will cover $50,000 in bodily injury up to $100,000 per accident.

Period 2 – You have accepted a request but do not yet have the passenger in the car.

---

[2]https://www.bloomberg.com/news/articles/2016-05-31/inside-uber-s-auto-lease-machine-where-almost-anyone-can-get-a-car.

[3]Ibid.

Uber and Lyft will provide collision insurance with a $1,000 deductible for Uber and $2,500 for Lyft.

Period 3 – You have a passenger in the car.

The same as Period 2[4] plus Uber will cover up to $1 million in bodily injury per accident in the event the driver's insurance won't cover the liability as well as $1 million in uninsured motorist coverage.[5]

If you are going to drive for Uber, you *must* get rideshare insurance. This is not required by Uber, but I'm telling you it's a necessity.

If you do not have rideshare insurance and get into an accident while driving, your insurance company will not cover the costs of the crash and will likely drop you. If you lie about having a customer in the car, that's insurance fraud and the consequences could be severe.

Rideshare insurance is likely to cost you from $113 per month to more than $200 per month.[6]

An extra $200 per month means a driver will have to drive for about 10 hours just to cover his or her rideshare insurance. So it's not hard to see why only 23% of Uber drivers carry the extra insurance.[7]

As a customer, you don't have to worry. If you get into an accident, Uber's policy will cover you up to $1 million.

But as a driver, if you get into an accident without a passenger in the car (Periods 1 and 2), there is a minimal amount of coverage and you could be on the hook for a big out-of-pocket expense.

When I said you *must* get rideshare insurance, I didn't mean that it's the law. You can drive without it. But from a risk perspective, it is crazy to pick up a part-time job to make a few hundred or even a few thousand bucks a month and risk everything you've worked your whole life for, if you get into an accident without proper insurance.

I would not suggest driving for Uber unless you can afford the extra insurance. It's just not worth it.

Expenses

As an Uber driver you are an independent contractor. You pay for gas, maintenance, insurance, and all costs related to your vehicle.

---

[4]http://time.com/money/4482057/heres-what-you-need-to-know-about-insuring-yourself-with-uber.

[5]https://newsroom.uber.com/insurance-for-uberx-with-ridesharing.

[6]http://theshareguy.com/how-much-does-rideshare-insurance-cost.

[7]http://www.insurancejournal.com/news/national/2016/02/29/400223.htm.

Keep track of your receipts carefully. If you burn through a tank of gas driving customers around town on a Saturday night, the cost of the gas can be taken off your taxes as a business expense.

Another important expense to track closely is how many miles you drive – and that includes driving to pick up a passenger or to go to a prime waiting spot. In 2017, the IRS allowed drivers a $0.535 per mile deduction for every mile you drive for business purposes.[8]

So if you drove 500 miles and earned $1,000, you'd only pay taxes on $732.50 in income (500 × 0.535 = 267.50. Then 1,000 – 267.50 = $732.50). And that's before tolls, insurance, and other related costs. You cannot deduct gas expenses if you're deducting mileage.

What Type of Car?

Most Uber drivers drive for the UberX service. These tend to be smaller, fuel-efficient cars like Toyota Priuses and Hyundai Sonatas.

If you have a minivan or SUV, you can drive for UberXL. It must be able to seat six passengers in addition to the driver. Riders are charged more for UberXL, so as a driver you'll make more, but your costs are higher with the larger, less fuel-efficient vehicle.

If you have a really nice car like a BMW 5 Series or Mercedes E Class, you can drive for Uber Black. This is more like a professional limousine service and charges the highest rates.

If you want to drive for Uber Black, your car should be in great condition and immaculate. You also must have a TCP permit or livery license.

Unless you're a professional driver, you probably don't want a bunch of strangers in your new Cadillac anyway.

If you're driving for UberX or UberXL, your car doesn't have to be immaculate, but it should be clean and not smell bad. A stinky and disgusting car is a sure way to get low ratings.

The rideshare industry has provided income to a lot of people who need flexibility or don't want to be tied to a schedule. There are costs involved and if you're going to make good money doing it, you're going to need to hustle.

But it's possible to make a few extra bucks each week to cover your greens fees and dinners out or to supplement your Social Security

---

[8]https://www.irs.gov/uac/2017-standard-mileage-rates-for-business-and-medical-and-moving-announced.

and other income. You'll work when you want to for as long as you want to and where you want to.

You never have to accept a passenger that you're not comfortable with and you might even meet some interesting people.

I use Uber often and usually try to talk to the driver about their experience. No one is getting rich off of it, and most people I've met drive in addition to another job, are in school, or are retired. But most of them said they like driving for Uber and are making what they were told to expect.

And don't think you'll be the only one your age driving to make some extra income. Twenty-three percent of Uber's drivers are older than 50.[9]

Resources

If you Google Uber, Lyft, or Ridesharing, there are a ton of resources on the web to help you learn more about it, including Uber and Lyft's websites.

The best site that I found is www.therideshareguy.com. Most of the information on the site is free including new driver guides, information about getting paid, expenses and links to sources for insurance, and helpful apps.

If you're considering becoming a driver, definitely check out The Rideshare Guy first.

Hopefully, you don't have to drive for Uber in retirement. But if you want to, there is money to be made.

Actions to Take

- If you're interested in driving for Uber, read The Ride Share Guy and Uber or Lyft's websites to be sure you have a complete understanding of the business.
- Consider rideshare insurance. It could protect you in a big way.
- Keep track of every mile you drive and every penny you spend when you're driving for Uber. You can write it off your taxes.
- Get the week-old tuna sandwich out of your car unless you want a low rating.

---

[9]http://www.cnbc.com/2016/09/30/uber-lyft-helps-seniors-cruise-into-retirement
.html.

CHAPTER 7

The 401k You've Never Heard Of

"Health Savings Accounts (HSAs) are the greatest employment benefit since the eight-hour workday."

– Me

If you're not yet on Medicare, this chapter may have the biggest impact on your finances.

When I discovered this little trick (before writing the book), I was so pumped I was jumping up and down.

Okay, maybe I get a little too excited about personal finance. But this is a big one, believe me.

It's a way to increase your retirement savings by 38% or more and get a sizable tax break while doing so.

I'm talking about Health Savings Accounts (HSAs).

Even if you think you know about HSAs, keep reading. You may not understand just how powerful this savings tool is.

HSAs are available for people that have high deductible health insurance policies. In 2018, "high deductible" is defined as a minimum deductible of $1,350 for individuals and $2,700 for families.[1]

---

[1] https://www.irs.gov/pub/irs-drop/rp-17-37.pdf.

HSAs are not the same as Flex Spending Accounts (FSAs). Employer sponsored FSAs can be used to pay medical or dependent care expenses depending on your plan. Like an HSA, money is put aside pre-tax. However, an FSA is a use it or lose it proposition. If you don't spend the money in a given year, it's gone. So you should only contribute what you know you're going to spend. Contributions to an HSA remain in your account until you use it, no matter how long it takes.

Having a higher deductible saves you money on your premiums. But obviously if you have some medical expenses, you'll pay those costs before your insurance kicks in.

By giving you a tax benefit, the HSA is designed to make it attractive for you to save money to cover health expenses.

We're not yet into the part about how it can act like an extension of your 401k – more on that in a minute. First, let's talk about the tax benefit.

Taxes

HSAs are *triple* tax advantaged. It lowers your taxable income, grows tax-free, and can be withdrawn tax-free.

Similar to a 401k, money that you contribute to an HSA is deducted from your paycheck pre-tax and is subtracted from your taxable income. That lowers the amount of tax you owe.

For example, if you earn $75,000 and contribute $5,000 to an HSA, your taxable income is now $70,000. If you're in the 25% tax bracket, you now owe the IRS $1,250 less than you would if you hadn't made the contribution ($5,000 * 25% = $1,250).

If you have money in your HSA when you die, the account is added to your estate and may be taxable unless your spouse is the beneficiary. If a spouse is the beneficiary, the account becomes his or her HSA and is not considered part of the estate or subject to taxes.[2]

---

[2]https://www.irs.gov/publications/p969/ar02.html#en_US_2016_publink1000 204096.

So just like a 401k, you've saved money and received a tax break for doing so.

Should you incur a healthcare-related cost, you can use the funds in the account to pay for the expense. You can pay directly from the account if you have a debit/credit card connected to your HSA or pay for the expense yourself and get reimbursed – up to the amount that is in your account.

HSAs cover a wide variety of health-related costs including co-pays, deductibles, and prescriptions. HSA funds can also be used for qualified medical expenses like orthodontic work (braces), guide dogs, vasectomy, pregnancy test kits, hearing aids, wheelchairs, contact lenses, addiction treatment, and so on.[3]

Having money in an HSA can be helpful if you get hit with a large unexpected medical cost. And that's what most people use it for.

But you're not most people.

Here's how you can use an HSA to ramp up your retirement savings and treat it like an extra 401k.

With most HSA plans, instead of keeping it in cash, you can invest the funds.

Now, if you plan on using the HSA to pay for medical bills in the near future, I don't advise investing the money. As I always tell my readers, don't invest any funds that you need in the next three years. If that investment loses value, you won't have the money available to pay your expenses.

So if you are going to use the HSA the way it was really intended – to pay for medical costs as they arise, keep the money in cash (money market). You won't earn much interest, but you won't lose anything either.

But if you want to treat your HSA like an IRA or 401k, you can invest the money. I suggest choosing solid long-term investments like quality index funds, or if you have the option, dividend growth stocks as described in Chapter 1.

This is a long-term strategy. Stocks and mutual funds can go down if there's a correction or bear market. But if you're treating it as a retirement savings vehicle, it's the same strategy as your 401k, except with more flexibility and greater benefits.

Let's say you're putting money away in your HSA and investing but then something terrible happens. You have an accident that will

---

[3]http://www.hsabank.com/~/media/files/eligible_medical_expenses.

cost you a great deal out of pocket. If you need to, you can dip into your HSA with no problem.

If you're fortunate to avoid a costly medical situation or have the funds to pay for it without tapping your HSA, once you turn 65, you can use the money for whatever you want – not just health-related costs.

However, it's better to use it for qualified medical expenses.

Once you hit 65 years of age, if you take funds out of your HSA for other expenses unrelated to healthcare costs, you will be taxed on the money, just like you will when you take money out of your 401k.

But there is no penalty for doing so.

If you take money out of the HSA before 65 for non-medical costs, it is subject to taxes, plus a whopping 20% penalty. So you really don't want to do that. After taxes and with a 20% penalty, you'll lose half of the money.

After 65, there is no 20% penalty. You'll just pay regular income taxes.

But that's only if it's not a qualified medical expense.

If you withdraw the funds for a qualified medical expense, you don't pay taxes or penalties.

So you can save for retirement with a huge immediate tax bene-fit, withdraw the money for anything you want after age 65, and just pay income tax on the funds; or use the money to pay for medical expenses and pay no taxes at all.

Plus, if you invest it wisely, the money is growing year after year. There is no reason why you can't double or triple those funds in ten years.

So the $5,000 you put away tax-free today could be worth $10,000 or $15,000 in ten years – also tax-free to pay for your healthcare.

Considering the average couple will spend $260,000 in out-of-pocket healthcare expenses in their lifetime, it's a no-brainer to sock money away now – particularly if it lowers your taxes today and is tax-free when you take it out in retirement to pay for healthcare costs.

I now put the maximum $6,900 per year in my HSA. It lowers my taxes by more than $2,000, which is a heck of a savings and will grow tax-free until I need it when I'm older.

If I do that for only five years and save $34,500 (it will likely be more as the maximum allowed savings typically increases every year or so), in 10 to 15 years I should have around $100,000 that I can withdraw tax-free for medical costs.

Medicare

Once you enroll in Medicare at age 65, you can no longer contribute to an HSA, but that doesn't mean the fun has to stop. You can use your HSA funds to pay your Medicare premiums.

This is an unusual feature: Before age 65, you cannot use your HSA money to pay for insurance premiums. (That said, as I write this, there is talk of proposed legislation to allow insurance premiums to be paid out of HSA funds. That could be allowed by the time you read this.) But remember, once you enroll in Medicare, you can pay your premiums out of your HSA account, new legislation or not.

How to Find an HSA

Many people have HSAs through their employers. If your employer does not offer one but you are still eligible, go online and do some research. You'll want to look for HSAs that have the best investment options and the lowest fees.

Morningstar published a study of the 10 largest HSA plans. For customers taking the long-term approach and investing the funds, it found the top three plans were:

1. Health Equity – www.healthequity.com
2. Optum Bank – www.optumbank.com
3. The HSA Authority – www.thehsaauthority.com

If you're using the HSA to cover healthcare costs as they arise – meaning you will not be investing the money – you'll want the plans with the lowest costs.

Morningstar identified the following HSA plans as having no monthly maintenance fees:

1. Alliant Credit Union – www.alliantcreditunion.org
2. The HSA Authority – www.hsaauthority.com
3. SelectAccount – www.selectaccount.com

There are others, some offered by banks you may already be doing business with. Check with them to see if they offer a better deal than the ones mentioned.

If you decide that a high deductible health plan is right for you, open an HSA right away to go along with it.

If you don't, you're needlessly sending money to the IRS that could be used for your healthcare expenses or retirement savings.

And when you do open that HSA, do your absolute best to let the money grow for as long as you can.

You can see now why I was so excited: Triple tax advantages and the ability to grow the money with the flexibility to be able to use it in an emergency if necessary? It's tough to find a better vehicle to help you plan for retirement.

Actions to Take

- If you have a high deductible insurance plan and are not on Medicare, open an HSA right now.
- If you can, name your spouse as a beneficiary to avoid taxes after you die.
- Invest the money for the long term to grow your retirement savings.
- Okay, maybe I'm a personal finance geek, but you have to admit, this HSA as a 401k thing is pretty exciting.

II

Cutting Costs

"Those who attend to small expenses are always rich"

– John Adams

No one ever *wants* to cut costs.

Frankly, it's not fun to be careful with your spending. What is fun is spoiling yourself or the people you care about.

And while the tips in the first section of this book should help generate some solid income for you, life gets expensive, particularly the older we get.

Healthcare costs are going higher every year. Despite our extremely competent and committed lawmakers in Washington (sorry, my sarcasm font isn't working), healthcare is going to continue to get more expensive.

So it makes sense to lower expenses where you can.

As I mentioned in the introduction, this book is about not compromising your lifestyle in retirement. I'm not going to suggest you stop going out to dinner or enjoying yourself.

But I will provide you with some tips that can shave a few bucks off of everyday spending and big expenses – with minimum effort. I promise that if you expend any time or energy on these methods, it will be worth it.

Many of these tactics will take 30 seconds or less to incorporate, yet can add up to real money over time. And the few that take a little more time can save you thousands of dollars all at once.

These moneysaving techniques will help stretch your dividend or other income, give you a greater sense of financial comfort, and help alleviate any guilt or hesitation you may have about enjoying your life in retirement.

According to the U.S. Bureau of Labor Statistics, the average retired household spends $40,938 per year.[1] So if we can cut a few hundred to a few thousand off that number, that's going to go a long way to extending your finances and making you more comfortable about a night out at a fancy restaurant.

So let's get right to it and start reducing your costs in a quick and painless way.

---

[1] http://money.usnews.com/money/retirement/slideshows/the-high-costs-of-the-retirement-dream.

CHAPTER 8

Lower Your Medicare Costs

"I'm too young for Medicare and too old for women to care."

– Kinky Friedman

If the idea of do-it-yourself surgery doesn't excite you (no, that's not a chapter in this book), there are other ways you can lower your healthcare costs. And you should try. As I mentioned earlier, the average retired couple will spend $260,000 in their lifetime on healthcare.

Medicare certainly helps, though if you end up in the hospital for a long stay and don't have secondary insurance, the costs will add up quickly.

If you have Medicare and are in the hospital, the first sixty days are on Uncle Sam. After that, you pay $335 per day for the next month. At 90 days, the bill goes up to $670 per day.[1] You could stay at the Four Seasons for less. So try to get out of the hospital quickly. These figures are for 2018. They will probably be higher in future years.

The most important thing you can do to save money on Medicare is sign up on time.

Your Medicare coverage starts when you turn 65. You can enroll between three months before the month of your 65th birthday and three months after the month you turn 65. So if your birthday is May 9th, you can sign up starting February 1st and as late as August 30th.

---

[1] https://www.cms.gov/Newsroom/MediaReleaseDatabase/Fact-sheets/2017-Fact-Sheet-items/2017-11-17.html.

If you don't sign up during this window, you will likely end up paying more for various plans including Medicare Part B, which covers doctor's visits; Part C, which is Medicare Advantage; Part D, which is prescriptions; Part F, which is a Medigap policy; and others.

In fact, for every 12 months you go without coverage, your Part B premiums will increase by 10%.[2]

Signing up late will raise your prescription drug premiums too. If you go 63 days without coverage, your premium for Part D, which covers prescription medication, goes up 1% times the number of months you are without coverage.

So if you wait until your 66th birthday, you'll pay 12% more for drug coverage than you'd need to.[3]

Fill the Gap

You definitely want to consider a supplemental insurance plan, also known as Part F and Medigap. This is a secondary insurance plan.

You'll have to pay a premium, so that could add to your costs. Like any insurance policy, you hope you never need it and are flushing money down the toilet. I'll be thrilled if I never have to use my homeowners, auto, health, and life insurance policies. I hope I'm an extremely profitable customer for my insurance company.

If you buy a Medigap policy and don't use it, that means you're healthy, so don't complain about wasted premiums.

But considering that Medicare beneficiaries are on the hook for 20% of their healthcare expenses, having a supplemental policy if you get really sick can be a financial lifesaver.

Imagine, God forbid, that you get cancer and need a $150,000 treatment, plus other costs. Without a supplemental policy you'll pay $30,000, plus 20% of your other costs.

A stroke, diabetes, and other serious diseases can drain your assets very quickly if you don't have protection.

To lower your premium costs, shop around and look for a high deductible plan. That way you're covered in case of a catastrophe or chronic serious illness, but aren't wasting money on premiums that you may not need.

A Part F plan may be the most expensive but offers the most benefits. A high deductible Plan F policy could cost as little as

---

[2]http://money.cnn.com/2017/05/01/pf/retirement-costs.
[3]Ibid.

$50 per month, depending on where you live, but the deductible is $2,240 in 2018.

If you have a second home, compare rates for both addresses. You can get your rate adjusted if you move to another area. So if you relocate to a cheaper location (Florida from New York, for example), make sure to get the break in your premium that you're entitled to.

Currently, if you sign up during the open enrollment period, a Medigap provider cannot charge you more because of a pre-existing condition or your age. They are permitted to do so if you miss the open enrollment window. So make sure you sign up during the open enrollment period.

When is that?

Anytime in the first six months starting the first day of the month after you are 65 and enrolled in Medicare Part B.[4] Remember, you can enroll in Medicare Part B in the three months before you turn 65, the month you turn 65 or the three months after you turn 65.

So if you turn 65 in May, but don't enroll in Medicare until June 30th, your Medigap open enrollment period would begin on July 1st.

Of course, with health insurance being such a political football, things could be different by the time you read this, or in a year or two.

Medicare Advantage

Medicare Advantage, or Part C, has some great benefits but limitations as well.

There are no out-of-pocket maximums. So if you get really sick and run up huge bills, the insurance provider can't cut you off.

On the other hand, private insurance companies provide the coverage. As a result, their network of healthcare providers may be limited. If you want to be sure you can see specific doctors, check if they are on any plan before you sign up. You may also be required to be referred to a specialist by your primary care doctor.

Generally, I'm not a big fan of insurance brokers. I know there are many good ones out there. I just haven't met too many. They're always trying to sell me coverage I don't need.

However, working with a broker who is an expert in Medicare and Medicare Advantage could save you thousands of dollars if he or she puts you in the right plan.

---

[4]https://medicare.com/medicare-supplement/when-can-you-buy-a-medigap-policy.

Ask friends and relatives for referrals. And be sure that the broker works with a variety of companies so they can find a policy for your unique needs. If the broker only represents one company, your options are limited and you may be pressured to buy the plan that they're pushing that month – in other words, the one that will pay the most commission.

Fight For Your Rights

Medicare makes mistakes.

To be fair, there are 68,000 diagnostic codes and 87,000 procedure codes,[5] so the likelihood something is mislabeled or coded wrong is quite high.

When you receive your quarterly statements from Medicare, look over them like you would any other financial statement. If there's a mistake, but you never look at your statements, that's your problem.

Go over your statements and make sure everything is correct. If not, you need to fight for your rights by filing an appeal.

And there's a chance you'll have to. In 2010, Medicare processed 906 billion claims and denied roughly 90 billion of them.[6] That's a lot of ticked off people that expected their drug, procedure, or other healthcare to be covered.

The good news is roughly half of appeals are reversed. In 2010, 43% of Medicare Part A denials and 53% of Part B denials were ultimately approved.[7]

Mail a letter or send an email explaining why you believe the denial was wrong. It may take persistence on your part, but stick with it and get what you're owed. It could be worth a lot of money.

Where to Get Help

If you file an appeal with Medicare and don't get satisfaction, there are agencies that will help you.

---

[5]https://www.acr.org/Advocacy/Economics-Health-Policy/Billing-Coding/Prepare-Now-for-ICD10.

[6]http://www.reuters.com/article/us-column-miller-medicare-idUSBRE8AC16F.20121113

[7]Ibid.

State Health Insurance Programs (SHIPs) offer free local personalized counseling programs to help you understand your benefits and file appeals. Visit www.shiptacenter.org for details.

The Medicare Rights Center is another nonprofit that offers free advice to seniors regarding Medicare. You can get more information on their website at www.medicarerights.org.

There are some excellent resources online to help you keep up with the rules and the various types of plans, their costs, and benefits – starting, believe it or not, with Medicare's website at www.medicare.gov.

Consumer Reports is also a good place to do your research.

The Best Way to Lower Your Costs

Lastly, it sounds obvious, but try to be healthy. Eat right, exercise, practice stress management. Not just because it's good for you, but it's cheaper. Medicare enrollees who are in poor health pay 2.5 times more out of pocket than their healthier peers.[8]

The Centers for Disease Control estimates that an overweight person who loses just 10% of their weight will reduce their lifetime medical costs by as much as $5,300.[9]

Think you're saving money by staying at home and sitting on the couch? Inactivity costs individuals between $670 and $1,125 per year in healthcare expenses.[10]

And here's an amazing statistic. If Americans ate just one more serving of fruits or vegetables per day, it would save 30,000 lives and lower medical costs by $5 billion.[11]

So an apple a day really can keep the doctor away.

The best way to keep your healthcare costs down are to not need a doctor.

You don't have to make radical changes to your lifestyle. Go for a walk after dinner; eat more fruits and vegetables. Not only will you feel better, but you'll save money on preventable healthcare costs.

---

[8]http://host.madison.com/business/investment/markets-and-stocks/jaw-dropping-stats-about-medicare/article_ff4b94f4-5663-5f5a-b180-57d7eb46f716.html.

[9]https://njaes.rutgers.edu/healthfinance/health-behaviors.asp.

[10]Ibid.

[11]http://www.ucsusa.org/food_and_agriculture/solutions/expand-healthy-food-access/11-trillion-reward.html#.WYdQ-601RPM.

Actions to Take

- Sign up for Medicare on time – between three months before the month of your 65th birthday and three months after the month you turn 65.
- Sign up for Medigap insurance during your open enrollment period – within six months of turning 65 and enrolling in Medicare Part B.
- Watch your statements and file appeals when denied.
- Your mother was right; eat more fruits and vegetables.

CHAPTER

Medical Tourism

"If you had your life to live over again, do it overseas."

– Henny Youngman

Everyone knows how expensive healthcare is in the United States. A pill that costs $7 in Canada or Europe could easily be in the hundreds of dollars in the good ole' U.S. of A.

The same goes for medical procedures.

Which is why an increasing number of people are going to other countries to get surgeries or other medical care.

Even if your insurance or Medicare won't cover a treatment in a foreign country, it can still be cheaper than receiving it in the U.S. – after deductibles and co-pays are taken into account.

Additionally, some patients travel abroad to undergo treatments that are not approved in the U.S.

Traveling to another country for medical treatment conjures images of being in a dirty, third world backwater clinic, while a quasi-qualified, eccentric doctor makes big promises for curing lethal diseases.

That's not reality for most patients.

Most medical tourists are treated in clean, top-of-the-line facilities by professional staff and have excellent outcomes at a fraction of the price.

More than 11 million people travel each year to be treated by doctors in other countries. It is a $100 billion industry that is forecast to grow 25% annually through 2025.[1]

---

[1] https://www.medicaltourismindex.com/wp-content/uploads/2016/07/MTA_1359_INFOGRAPH.jpg.

According to the Medical Tourism Index, the top five destinations are:

1. Canada
2. U.K.
3. Singapore
4. Israel
5. Germany

And the top five countries in terms of quality of facilities and services are:

1. Israel
2. Germany
3. India
4. Canada
5. U.K.[2]

It's big business. Do a Google News search for "medical tourism" and you'll see lots of articles emanating from a variety of countries as they try to promote their medical tourism industry:

"Push to Promote Abu Dhabi as Medical Tourism Destination" – *The National*[3]

"Medical Tourism: Just What the Doctor Ordered for India" – *Khaleej Times*[4]

"Costa Rica Has New Medical Tourism Promotional Body" – *The Costa Rica Star*[5]

Risks

Keep in mind that with any medical treatments or procedures, there are risks. And those risks are exacerbated by being in a foreign country. Not because the quality of care is lower but because you are far away from home.

---

[2]https://www.medicaltourismindex.com/wp-content/uploads/2016/07/MTA_1359_INFOGRAPH.jpg.

[3]http://www.thenational.ae/business/travel-tourism/push-to-promote-abu-dhabi-as-medical-tourism-destination.

[4]http://www.khaleejtimes.com/travel/medical-tourism-just-what-the-doctor-prescribed-for-india.

[5]http://news.co.cr/costa-rica-has-new-medical-tourism-promotional-body/59859.

If you have a problem, friends and family that you might want close to you may not be able to get to you right away.

Some infectious diseases may be more common in other countries than in the U.S. There could be some language barriers (though if the doctor/hospital/facility caters to medical tourists that shouldn't be as big of a concern). And the postoperative care could be very different from what is standard in the U.S.

Should something go wrong, your legal remedies also will be different. The fact that litigation is somewhat limited in many countries is one of the reasons why costs are so much lower.

So if the doctor replaces your left knee instead of your right, you may simply be out of luck.

The blood supply may also be a concern. Talk to the doctor that will perform the surgery to understand where the hospital gets its blood, in case you need an infusion. Do they screen for HIV or other infections? That is something you definitely want to know if there's any chance you'll need blood.

Depending on the procedure, you may not be able to just hop on a plane home as soon as you're discharged. You may need to recover in a hotel room for a few days or weeks. So you need to be comfortable doing that in a foreign country if you're going to opt for medical care outside the United States.

I once had to stay in a hotel in New Jersey for two days after a procedure, and I was miserable. Of course, that might have had more to do with the fact that I was in New Jersey than the medical procedure. Ba-*dum*-bum.

But seriously, if you're going to be recuperating after surgery, you want to ensure you're comfortable wherever you are. This is not the time for being adventurous and staying in a cheap motel on the outskirts of town.

Stay in the nicest hotel you can afford that is closest to your medical facility.

Cost

If you do opt for medical care overseas, the cost savings can be significant.

For example, a knee replacement that costs $35,000 in the U.S. costs $6,600 in India, $17,500 in South Korea, and $16,000 in Singapore.

Medical procedure	USA	Costs Rica	Colombia	India	Jordan	S. Korea	Mexico	Israel	Thailand	Vietnam	Malaysia	Poland	Singapore	Turkey
Heart Bypass	$123,000	$27,000	$14,800	$7,900	$14,400	$26,000	$27,000	$28,000	$15,000		$12,100	$14,000	$17,200	$13,900
Angioplasty	$28,200	$13,800	$7,100	$5,700	$5,000	$17,700	$10,400	$7,500	$4,200		$8,000	$5,300	$13,400	$4,800
Heart Valve Replacement	$170,000	$30,000	$10,450	$9,500	$14,400	$39,900	$28,200	$28,500	$17,200		$13,500	$19,000	$16,900	$17,200
Hip Replacement	$40,364	$13,600	$8,400	$7,200	$8,000	$21,000	$13,500	$36,000	$17,000	$9,250	$8,000	$5,500	$13,900	$13,900
Hip Resurfacing	$28,000	$13,200	$10,500	$9,700	$9,000	$19,500	$12,500	$20,100	$13,500		$12,500	$9,200	$16,350	$10,100
Knee Replacement	$35,000	$12,500	$7,200	$6,600	$9,500	$17,500	$12,900	$25,000	$14,000	$8,000	$7,700	$8,200	$16,000	$10,400
Spinal Fusion	$110,000	$15,700	$14,500	$10,300	$10,000	$16,900	$15,400	$33,500	$9,500	$6,150	$6,000	$6,200	$12,800	$16,800
Dental Implant	$2,500	$800	$1,200	$900	$900	$1,350	$900	$1,200	$1,720		$1,500	$925	$2,700	$1,100
Lap Band	$14,000	$9,450	$8,500	$7,300	$7,000	$10,200	$6,500	$17,300	$11,500		$8,150	$6,700	$9,200	$8,600
Gastric Sleeve	$16,500	$11,500	$11,200	$6,000	$7,500	$9,950	$8,900	$20,000	$9,900		$8,400	$9,400	$11,500	$12,900
Gastric Bypass	$25,000	$12,900	$12,200	$7,500	$7,500	$10,900	$11,500	$24,000	$16,800		$9,900	$9,750	$13,700	$13,800
Hysterectomy	$15,400	$6,900	$2,900	$3,200	$6,600	$10,400	$4,500	$14,500	$3,650		$4,200	$2,200	$10,400	$7,000
Breast Implants	$6,400	$3,500	$2,500	$3,000	$4,000	$3,800	$3,800	$3,800	$3,500	$4,000	$3,800	$3,900	$8,400	$4,500
Rhinoplasty	$6,500	$3,800	$4,500	$2,400	$2,900	$3,980	$3,800	$4,600	$3,300	$2,100	$2,200	$2,500	$2,200	$3,100
Face Lift	$11,000	$4,500	$4,000	$3,500	$3,950	$6,000	$4,900	$6,800	$3,950	$4,150	$3,550	$4,000	$440	$6,700
Liposuction	$5,500	$2,800	$2,500	$2,800	$1,400	$2,900	$3,000	$2,500	$2,500	$3,000	$2,500	$1,800	$2,900	$3,000
Tummy Tuck	$8,000	$5,000	$3,500	$3,500	$4,200	$5,000	$4,500	$10,900	$5,300	$3,000	$3,900	$3,550	$4,650	$4,000
Lasik (both eyes)	$4,000	$2,400	$2,400	$1,000	$4,900	$1,700	$1,900	$3,800	$2,310	$1,720	$3,450	$1,850	$3,800	$1,700
Cornea (per eye)	$17,500	$9,800	N/A	$2,800	$5,000	N/A	N/A	N/A	$3,600		N/A	N/A	$9,000	$7,000
Cataract surgery (per eye)	$3,500	$1,700	$1,600	$1,500	$2,400	N/A	$2,100	$3,700	$1,800		$3,000	$750	$3,250	$1,600
IVF Treatment	$12,400	N/A	$5,450	$2,500	$5,000	$7,900	$5,000	$5,500	$4,100		$6,900	$4,900	$14,900	$5,200

Source: MedicalTourism.com

Dental implants that would set you back $2,500 if you had them put in by an American dental surgeon would only be $800 if done in Costa Rica.

In the table, you can see the cost difference of 21 procedures in 14 countries as of 2016.

These costs do not include flights or extended hotel stays.

Accreditation

The Joint Commission International (JCI) is a nonprofit organization that evaluates and accredits healthcare organizations around the world. There are other accrediting agencies, but JCI is considered the gold standard.

JCI accreditation means the facility meets U.S. standards, though accommodations are made for cultural differences.

There are currently 945 accredited facilities for a variety of conditions.[6] You can search JCI's website for specific diseases to see which accredited facilities are up to standards.

Resources

If you're considering going abroad for healthcare, be sure to thoroughly do your homework on the doctor, facility, country, and all of the other variables that will be different than if you get taken care of in your town or city.

Fortunately, there are many online resources to help you.

I'd start with **JCI**. If a hospital is not accredited by JCI, that should be a deal breaker.

I'm sure there are good healthcare facilities that are not accredited, but why chance it? If it has JCI accreditation, you at least know that it has the same standards as a U.S. hospital.

Patients Beyond Borders – You can use its website to look up hospitals by condition that you're interested in and by region or country.

Let's say you wanted to combine a vacation in Southeast Asia with liposuction surgery (many people will do some sightseeing before their procedure).

Patients Beyond Borders recommends eight facilities in Thailand, Malaysia, and Singapore. The description of the facility

---

[6]http://www.jointcommissioninternational.org/about-jci/jci-accredited-organizations.

will usually tell you if it's JCI accredited. If not, you can always go to the JCI site to cross reference.

In this example, Bumrungrad International Hospital in Bangkok, Thailand, was one of the choices. The description mentions that it was the first hospital in Thailand to achieve JCI accreditation.

Checking the JCI website confirms that it is accredited.

Not every recommendation on the Patients Beyond Borders site is JCI accredited. But again, I'd stick to only facilities that have achieved the JCI accreditation to be safe.

In many cases, there will be a "Related Patient Stories" section on the Patients Beyond Borders hospital site that details a real patient's experience at the hospital.

In the Bumrungard International example, two patients – Bruce from Florida and Trish from North Carolina – describe their treatments at the hospital.

The **Medical Tourism Association**'s website at www.medical tourism.com allows you to request a quote for various treatments including country preference.

International Medical Travel Journal lists hospitals, clinics, facilitators, agents, associations, government organizations, and other services such as air ambulances, holiday dialysis, and interpreters.

It also has a search function where you can research by type of care that is needed and country.

Going outside of the U.S. can be a cost effective way to receive treatment for a variety of conditions. It could save you thousands, or even tens of thousands of dollars.

Safety is the most important aspect. What good is saving a few thousand dollars if you wind up with a nasty infection that could kill you? So do your homework and thoroughly vet the doctors and facilities that you're considering working with.

Actions to Take

- Consider going abroad to save a lot of money on medical procedures.
- Only use a JCI-accredited facility.
- Spend the extra money to make sure you're comfortable while you recover, before you get on a plane home.
- Don't recuperate in New Jersey. (I'm just busting on Jersey. I received excellent care.)

10

Pay Less for Your Medicine

"I believe in prescription drugs. I believe in feeling better."

– Dennis Leary

A host of elected officials have promised to lower drug costs.

So far, about the only thing that has been done is to appoint a generic drug friendly head of the Food and Drug Administration (FDA) in 2017.

Dr. Scott Gottlieb has taken steps to bring generic drugs to market more quickly and increase competition among generic drug makers.

That should help. A little.

More than any other industry, the drug lobby owns Congress. And it's not going to take a "new system" that crushes their profits lying down.

Additionally, new therapies take many years and hundreds of millions of dollars to develop and bring to market. Investors, scientists, and executives need incentives to allocate their time, capital, and resources into researching these medicines. If the profit potential isn't there, new medicines will not be discovered.

We're still in a capitalist society and capitalism works – especially when it comes to discovering new medicines. How many groundbreaking therapies came out of the Soviet Union or Cuba?

So despite politicians' empty promises, drug prices are likely going to stay high for the foreseeable future.

But there are various ways you can drastically lower the cost of your prescriptions. In some cases you'll get your medicine free. And most of these services won't cost you anything.

GoodRx

You may be shocked to learn that the same medicine can cost hundreds of dollars more at one pharmacy than at another literally down the street.

GoodRx (www.goodrx.com) is a great site that shows you which pharmacies near you offer your medicine at the lowest price. GoodRx will also provide you with special discounts and coupons that you can use for extra savings.

The site is completely free.

I searched for the lowest prices on 30 tablets of depression fighter, Abilify, in Vinita, Oklahoma (prices vary depending on location). The cheapest was $59.70 if you bought it online at HealthWarehouse. If you want to pick up the prescription in person, it will cost you $248.84 at Wal-Mart and $297.98 at Walgreens, both with a coupon from GoodRx.

That's a significant difference.

If you're in New Rochelle, New York, and are taking Nexavar for kidney cancer, there is a $1,154 difference between the least and most expensive options.

When you sign up, if you mention that you have Medicare Part D or Advantage plans, it will show you the price you'll pay for a drug on your plan.

GoodRx even has discounts and coupons on medication for your pets.

You can download the GoodRx app on your phone so you can check prices when you have the prescription in hand on your way out of the doctor's office.

The site and app are very easy to use. Unless you have a relationship with your pharmacist that knows you and the various medications that you're taking, consider shopping around for the lowest price using GoodRx. You could save hundreds or even thousands of dollars a month.

Partnership for Prescription Assistance (PPA)

PPA (www.pparx.org) is a free service that helps patients without drug coverage to get reduced or free medicine.

It offers access to 475 programs including more than 200 biopharmaceutical companies. PPA has helped connect nearly 10 million patients, since it launched in 2005.

PPA also provides information on nearly 10,000 free healthcare clinics.

To use PPA, you fill out a questionnaire that does not require identifying personal information – though you do need to list which drugs you are taking, your income, and the type of insurance you have so that you can be matched to the right programs.

I filled out a questionnaire saying I lived in Florida, was 65 years old, and had an annual income of $100,000. I put in such a high income because I wanted to see if there were any programs for seniors that were doing well, but still facing high drug costs. I entered three drugs, including an expensive one for a rare disease.

It matched me up with a program called Serving Health Insurance Needs of Elders (SHINE), which is offered by the Florida Department of Elder Affairs. I would then have to call SHINE's number to see what they can do for me.

I entered another profile. This one was a 54-year-old patient in upstate New York, who was taking three drugs including two heart medicines. I said my household income was $60,000 per year and my insurance was an HMO with no drug coverage.

PPA matched me with RxOutreach, a nonprofit agency that helps provide affordable medication. I've seen other matches with programs run by the drug companies themselves that provide free medicine to those in need.

SimpleFill

SimpleFill (www.simplefill.com) charges $45 per month for help with one medication, $85 for two to five medications, $95 for six to eight, $105 to 11 and $115 for 12 or more.

You can also sign up to have SimpleFill help you manage a specific disease for $45 per month for nine months. SimpleFill guarantees you will get at least $2,000 in grants to use toward the specific disease, or you don't pay the $45 fee.

SimpleFill refunds all charges (except for a $10 processing fee) if the patient isn't approved for a program. It only accepts patients it believes has a 95% change of receiving a grant.

The other free services mentioned before provide you with resources, but you have to do all the work to get the reduced or free medicine. While you pay for SimpleFill, they take care of everything for you.

SimpleFill will provide personal advice on the best way to lower your drug costs, including helping you through the sign-up process with the various programs. Its monthly fees include:

- Finding the programs that will provide you with free or discounted medication
- Completing the program applications for the patient, with the exception of the signature
- Working directly with the doctor for their portion of the paperwork
- Automatically processing refills
- Contacting doctors when a new prescription is required

There are other free and fee-based programs that can help you cut your medication cost. Just do a Google search if the three just mentioned don't work for you.

There is no reason to pay full price for expensive medicines. Services are available to help you save hundreds of dollars or more per month on your medication.

You can also ask your doctor if there is a generic version of the branded medication that is being prescribed. If there is, ask if there is any reason not to take the generic instead. (Sometimes the generics are not identical to the branded drugs, nor have they been rigorously tested like the branded medicine.)

If the doctor says the generic is as safe and effective as the branded medication, ask for a prescription for the generic version. That could save you a lot of money.

Maybe that "new system" that the government pretends it's going to create will make services like these obsolete, and we'll all have cheap medicine.

But don't count on it.

Actions to Take

- Be a smart consumer. Comparison shop for your medication.
- See if you qualify for assistance programs.
- Ask your doctor if you can take a generic.
- Don't, I repeat, don't count on Washington to fix the high-cost-of-drugs problem.

CHAPTER

11

Pay Less in Taxes

"The only difference between death and taxes is that death doesn't get worse every time Congress meets."

– Will Rogers

I'm not breaking any news when I tell you that the government is deeply in debt. And I don't even know which country you live in. It probably doesn't matter.

As of 2014, there are only three independent countries on the planet that are not in debt – oil rich Brunei, Liechtenstein, and Palau.[1] Combined, the three countries have a population of less than half a million people.

Considering that my work isn't particularly popular in Brunei and Palau (I'm huge in Liechtenstein), chances are you're one of the other 7,584,636,000 people on the planet dwelling in a country that is in debt.

If you live in the U.S., your government owes trillions of dollars. The number of trillions depends on who you ask. The figure is so big the specifics almost don't matter.

What does matter is that the only way government can operate and even think about paying off that debt is by taxing its citizens. As a result, taxes are likely going higher, no matter what a politician promises or what new laws are passed. Remember, President George H.W. Bush's famous vow, "Read my lips. No new taxes"?

---

[1] http://www.therichest.com/rich-list/rich-countries/the-only-5-countries-in-the-world-living-debt-free.

Guess what happened shortly after that statement was made. You got it. New taxes.

Even if income taxes are lowered, new taxes will make up the difference.

But you don't have to pay more taxes than you're legally obliged. It is absolutely your right to find ways to save on taxes and pay as little as possible, as long as it's within the law.

Fortunately, there are lots of ways to lower taxes. Some of them are unconventional – but perfectly legal – and will reduce your tax bill by hundreds or even thousands of dollars a year.

Uncle Sam Will Pay You to Save

This one is one of the most shocking things I discovered when conducting research for this book. I double-checked that I was actually on an IRS website to make sure I wasn't being fooled. But it's true.

Depending on your income, you can receive a tax credit simply for saving money in an IRA or 401k.

Here's how it works.

If you are married and filing jointly and your adjusted gross income is less than $62,000, you can get a 10% to 50% tax credit from the IRS after contributing to a qualified retirement account.

2017 Saver's Credit			
Credit Rate	Married Filing Jointly	Head of Household	All Other Filers*
50% of your contribution	AGI not more than $37,000	AGI not more than $27,750	AGI not more than $18,500
20% of your contribution	$37,001–$40,000	$27,751–$30,000	$18,501–$20,000
10% of your contribution	$40,001–$62,000	$30,001–$46,500	$20,001–$31,000
0% of your contribution	more than $62,000	more than $46,500	more than $31,000

Source: Internal Revenue Service[2]

---

[2]https://www.irs.gov/retirement-plans/plan-participant-employee/retirement-savings-contributions-savers-credit?_ga=1.126673677.1266066666.1431525228.

Here's an example: You are retired and filing jointly. Your adjusted gross income is $50,000. You are young enough that you do not have to make the required minimum distribution from your IRA, so you contribute $2,000 to the IRA.

You are entitled to a 10% tax credit. As a result, you will pay $200 less in taxes.

This is an especially valuable credit if you are working. It's an incentive to save for retirement. Not only will you invest for the future, but you'll immediately get some money back in the form of tax savings. The Saver's Credit is not affected by the new tax law signed in December 2017.

The income limits go up annually, so be sure to check with the IRS each year to see what has changed.

Now, even if your income is above the level where you'll receive a tax credit, you should definitely save in a 401k or IRA if you can. Not only will the money grow tax deferred but it will lower your taxes.

Here's how:

Let's say you earn $100,000 per year and can afford to contribute $10,000 to a 401k. That $10,000 is pre-tax money. Meaning you will not be taxed on it. In fact, it reduces your taxable income by $10,000. So now, you will pay income tax on $90,000 instead of $100,000, saving about $2,500 in taxes if you're married filing jointly.

Not only is your $10,000 growing tax deferred, you're paying $2,500 less in taxes. That's $2,500 directly in your pocket instead of Uncle Sam's.

Traditional IRAs work the same way but have lower maximum contributions. So, you likely won't be able to contribute as much as $10,000.

The difference is an IRA contribution isn't made pre-tax, because it's not coming directly out of your paycheck, like a 401k contribution. But it still reduces your taxable income. If you contribute $5,000 to an IRA, it lowers your taxable income by $5,000. If you're in the 25% tax bracket, you'll save around $1,250.

Note, that Roth IRAs work differently. Your taxable income is not reduced by a contribution to a Roth IRA.

Check with the IRS or your accountant for the current maximum allowable contribution to an IRA. It usually goes up every year.

If you contribute to a 401k, the human resources department at your company should know what the maximum annual contribution is. In 2018, The maximum contribution is $18,500.

Charitable Giving

If you don't itemize your deductions but want to get a tax break for donating to charity, there's a way you can still save on your taxes.

If you are old enough to withdraw funds from an IRA or 401k, you can donate to charity with funds withdrawn from a retirement account tax-free.[3] (But note; this does not work with Roth IRAs.)

It could save you thousands in taxes.

Let's say you are going to withdraw $10,000 from your IRA this year and want to donate $1,000 to your favorite charity (or charities). You don't itemize, and you are in the 28% tax bracket.

If you donate the $1,000 with money from your plain old checking account, while it's a generous thing to do and you may get some karma points, there is no financial benefit. Remember, in this case, you're not itemizing.

If you donate that same $1,000 from your IRA, you pay tax on the other $9,000 you withdrew for yourself, but that $1,000 donation is exempt, saving you $280.

You still donated $1,000 to your favorite charity, but because you did it out of your IRA, you saved $280 in taxes.

So, if you're planning both a withdrawal from your retirement accounts and a charitable donation without itemizing, be sure to donate directly from your retirement accounts to lower your taxes.

Best of all, these charitable donations count toward the required minimum distribution that begins at age 70 1/2.

You can also use this technique outside of your retirement funds.

Let's say you have a large capital gain on a stock in your taxable account. You can donate the stock to the charity at the current market value and get the tax benefit.

For example, you bought 100 shares of stock at $25. It has now doubled to $50, giving you a profit of $2,500. Every year, you donate $1,000 to your favorite charity. Instead of writing a check, you can donate 20 shares of stock. You avoid capital gains taxes, and the charity still gets its donation from you.

Don't Pay Sales Tax Twice

You can legally deduct the sales tax you've paid from your federal income taxes if you don't claim state and local income taxes.

---

[3]https://www.irs.gov/uac/rda-2016-0122-2016-and-2016-form-1099r.

This will most likely apply to those in states with no state income tax, though it could apply to those with state income taxes if a big-ticket item (like a motor home or boat) is purchased.

States without state income tax are Alaska, Florida, Nevada, South Dakota, Texas, Washington, and Wyoming. Residents of Tennessee and New Hampshire may also get a benefit as those states tax investment income, but not wages.

Now it probably doesn't make sense to keep all your receipts from CVS showing that you paid 49 cents in sales tax on a pack of cough drops. But, if you're going to have some big expenses where you'll pay considerable sales tax, then it is.

I'm talking about things like a car, furniture, or artwork. In that case, hang on to those CVS receipts in addition to the receipts for the big-ticket items.

The good news is you don't have to hang on to all those receipts. You can use a simple formula to calculate your estimated sales tax. The formula is provided by the IRS for estimating your taxes by taking your gross income, number of dependents, and other variables into account.

For example, if you're a family making $100,000, living in Tampa, Florida, with two deductions you would have paid an estimated $1,159 in sales tax, according to the IRS. You would then be able to include that total in your itemized deductions.

The IRS Sales Tax Deduction Calculator can be found at www.irs.gov/individuals/sales-tax-deduction-calculator. Then, click on Sales Tax Calculator.

But if you do have those big-ticket items, you probably want to hang on to your documentation because the sales tax paid will likely be higher than the government formula.

To do that, you use IRS form Schedule A.

Note, the new tax reform law signed in December 2017 limits the amount of state and local income, property and sales tax deduction to $10,000.

Go Green

Tax credits are often available for renewable energy improvements to your home or for buying an electric car.

If you put a solar water heater in your house, you'll not only slash your electric bill, but you may be eligible for a tax credit that comes right off your taxes.

The Residential Energy Efficiency Tax Credit allows you to take a 30% credit on the expenses related to installing a solar water heater, solar electric system, fuel cells, wind energy, or geothermal heat pumps.

If you spend $10,000 on a solar electric system, you can take $3,000 right off your taxes.

Electric vehicle owners can take up to $7,500 in tax credits depending on the make and model of the car, but only until the manufacturer has sold 200,000 qualifying cars. Once that occurs, the credit will disappear.

Politics can affect these credits. Presidents and members of Congress may increase, decrease, or eliminate them depending on whose lobbyists donated the most.

Check with your accountant or the IRS to see if the tax credit is a factor in your decision whether to buy an electric vehicle or a renewable energy source for your home.

Can You Really Write Off Your Pool?

As of 2017 the IRS allowed you to write off medical expenses, including but not limited to expenses for hospital bills and drugs.

Alternative medicine such as acupuncture, massage, herbal remedies, and so on are usually allowable as a deduction.

And you may even be able to deduct the cost of a new pool in your backyard if it is primarily for therapeutic purposes. But you should be ready to prove to the IRS that you're only using it for a prescribed therapy – because chances are, they will challenge it.

At the time this book went to press, there were proposals in the House and Senate to eliminate this deduction as part of a tax reform bill. Check with your accountant to see if you still can write off medical costs.

Reinvested Dividends

If you know anything about me, you know that I love four things – boxing, The Rolling Stones, reinvesting dividends, and my family – and not necessarily in that order.

While I could write pages and pages about the Stones, the sweet science, and my kids, for your sake, I'll focus on reinvesting dividends.

It's my favorite investment strategy as outlined in Chapter 1. And many investors agree with me.

However, when it comes to their taxes, the same investors sometimes forget an important component of reinvesting dividends that could reduce their taxes.

When you reinvest your dividends in a stock or fund, you are buying more shares. If the stock rises over time, this adds to your cost basis and will reduce your capital gains.

Let's say you buy $5,000 worth of stock over the years and reinvest $1,000 worth of dividends. You sell all your shares for $12,000. Your capital gain is $6,000 because you initially paid $5,000 and bought another $1,000 worth of stock with your dividends.

But many investors fail to account for the reinvested dividends. They would say that because their initial purchase was for $5,000, their capital gain was $7,000 instead of $6,000. That error can cost you hundreds or thousands of dollars.

If you sold stock or shares of a mutual fund and have been reinvesting dividends, make absolutely sure that the capital gain reported on your tax forms that you receive from your broker or fund family includes reinvested dividends. If you're not sure, call them up and get an explanation or demand that they be included. They often are, but sometimes firms make mistakes, especially if you've owned the investment for years or it was transferred from another brokerage house.

Estate Taxes on a Retirement Account

If you had to pay estate taxes because you inherited a large sum of money and the estate included retirement funds, you are entitled to a tax credit equal to the amount of tax paid on the account.

For example, if the IRA had $50,000 in it and the heir was taxed $20,000 on it, that $20,000 can be deducted from the heir's taxes owed.

This is called estate tax on income in respect of a decedent.

If you're dealing with estate taxes, be sure you're working with a good accountant. He or she will be well worth their fee.

Jury Pay Paid to an Employer

I served on a jury. It was fascinating. I think I was paid $9 per day. Today, you might be able to get $15 per day. Maybe more.

That's not exactly going to bankroll your retirement. And in addition to inconveniencing you (yes, I know it's our civic duty, but not many people like it), Uncle Sam wants his cut. It doesn't matter that the jury pay didn't cover your lunch and parking.

You must declare income from jury duty on your taxes.

But if you are working and your employer pays your salary during jury duty, that jury pay gets turned over to your employer. However, you're still going to get a tax bill for it.

Because the jury pay was turned over to your company, be sure to take the deduction on line 36 of form 1040. There is no line for jury duty so you'll have to write it in.[4]

34	Tuition and fees. Attach Form 8917	34			
35	Domestic production activities deduction. Attach Form 8903	35			
36	Add lines 23 through 35 . **Jury duty pay**		36	9	00
37	Subtract line 36 from line 22. This is your **adjusted gross income** . . . . . ▶		37		

Source: Forbes[5]

It's a small amount, but why give the IRS a dollar more than you have to? That $9 you save could be spent on a couple of lattes. Just save your Starbucks receipt if you live in a state with no income tax.

Actions to Take

- Do whatever you can to put money in a 401k or IRA. Not only will the money grow tax deferred but it will also lower your income taxes in the current year.
- Donate stock or funds directly from your brokerage or retirement accounts in order to lower taxes on capital gains.
- Keep track of how much sales tax you paid if you buy big-ticket items during the year.
- Can you believe that after sitting in a room at the courthouse for a week, the IRS wants a piece of your $15 a day? Don't forget to declare it or take the deduction.

---

[4]https://apps.irs.gov/app/vita/content/17/17_08_005.jsp.

[5]http://www.forbes.com/sites/kellyphillipserb/2014/03/18/taxes-from-a-to-z-2014-j-is-for-jury-duty-pay/#535d771c34f3.

12

Lower Your Investment Costs

"If saving money is wrong, I don't want to be right."

– William Shatner

Very early in my career I used a financial advisor.

The advisor I used was a good guy. He was earnest in his attempt to generate solid returns without too much risk. I had no complaints about him and am friendly with him to this day.

But after working with him for a few years, it dawned on me I was paying him to basically rebalance my portfolio once a year. Sure, if I had intricate needs, he could have handled them. But I was paying 1% of my assets for him to set up a financial plan and then rebalance yearly.

That cost me thousands of dollars per year. After several years of this, it hit me how much I had spent and I closed the account.

I bought some index funds based on a sensible asset allocation model. The one I use is The Oxford Club's Gone Fishin' Portfolio created by Alexander Green. After that, I built a portfolio of Perpetual Dividend Raisers based on my 10-11-12 System.

I rebalance once a year and save thousands of dollars not paying an advisor. Those are dollars that stay in my portfolio and compound over the years, instead of winding up in an advisor's.

Let's take a look at how much money you can save managing your own money instead of paying an advisor 1% of your assets every year.

If you have a $500,000 portfolio that grows at a respectable, but nothing to get excited about, 8% per year, after 10 years you'd have $1,079,462. After 20 years, your nest egg would be $2,330,487.

However, if you're paying an advisor 1% of your assets, you wind up with $976,246 after 10 years and $1,906,114 after 20.

Over 10 years, you'll have paid $74,327 in fees. After 20, you'll have paid $219,451.

That is a lot of money that should be working for you. And you're not just out the money that went out the door. Because those funds were taken out of your account, they couldn't grow along with the rest of your investment capital.

So yes, you paid $74,327 over 10 years, but the difference in your account was more than $103,000. In 20 years, you paid $219,451 but the difference was more than $424,373.

$500K growing 8% per year	10 years	20 years
No advisor fee	$1,079,462	$2,330,487
1% advisor fee	$976,246	$1,906,114
Difference	$103,216	$424,373

Remember how we talked about compounding in Chapter 1? Well the same is true here, except it's working in reverse.

After one year of paying the 1% fee, you'll have $5,000 less that will compound at 8% over the years. After year two, there will be another $7,000 not compounding. And so on.

If you believe your financial advisor is giving you sound advice that you couldn't figure out on your own, or assists you with complicated matters like trusts and estate planning, or simply helps you sleep at night knowing a professional is watching your portfolio – than it's worth that 1% fee.

If handling the portfolio yourself is going to give you added stress or cause arguments with your spouse, it's worth paying the 1% to someone else.

But if you can handle your own investments – and it's my belief that most people can – then the easiest way to lower your investment costs is to stop paying a financial advisor.

Set yourself up with some index funds and some Perpetual Dividend Raisers and keep those thousands of dollars per year for yourself.

Keep in mind that not all advisors use index funds. Some may use more expensive funds or investments that further eat away at your returns.

If an advisor uses an actively managed mutual fund in your account, you're probably paying a 1% or higher expense ratio. An index fund likely has a 0.2% expense ratio, or lower.

And when you buy a stock like a Perpetual Dividend Raiser, it can cost you as little as $7. If you hold the stock for 10 years, as is my strategy, you know what it costs you?

Seven dollars.

Not per year, just $7 to buy it if you use a discount broker.

Let's say you took $100,000 and invested it in 10 stocks, paying $7 for each purchase. It would cost you $70 in commissions or 0.07%. After the first year, you make two trades a year costing you $14 per year. After 10 years, your total cost was $196 or 0.19% over ten years – an average of 0.019% per year. Now you're saving some money.

The big discount brokers like Ameritrade, Schwab, and E*Trade typically charge $7 per stock trade. Some discount brokers may go as high as $10.

If you're using a full service broker, it will cost you more. If you're not using the full service provided by the full service brokerage company, transfer your funds to one of the discount brokers and you'll save a lot of cash.

Plus, many discount brokers have offers for new accounts that include free trades. And not just one or two. I'm talking 100 or 200 free trades. It depends on the offer at the time.

The best part about these discount brokers is they don't charge you to hold your assets like a full service broker or financial advisor. So if you set up your account and didn't make any transactions for 10 years, you wouldn't pay a dime after those initial purchases.

Plus, many discount brokers allow you to buy mutual funds with no transaction costs.

It's possible; you could set up your entire portfolio with commission free index funds in a discount brokerage account and never pay a transaction cost or annual fee. How's that for low cost?

Pay a One-Time Fee

If you do want professional help, another option is to talk to a financial advisor who will charge you a one-time fee to create a plan for you. Most advisors will try to convince you to let them manage your account, but if you want only the initial plan, you can probably get it done for about $700. Then, you can set up the plan with one of the discount brokers.

Some discount brokers offer financial planning. For example, Vanguard charges just a 0.3% annual fee to set up a customized financial plan and provide ongoing financial advice. Schwab charges 0.28%.

Again, if you need assistance with complex account structures, trusts, insurance products, and taxes, a full service financial planner or advisor is probably the best course of action for you. But if you just need help with asset allocation and picking some mutual funds, index funds, or exchange-traded funds (ETFs), the financial planning services at some of the discount brokers will work just fine.

You could even use the planning service just for that first year, and then stop using (and paying for) it but still keep your account set up the way they recommended. Then, down the road if your needs change, use them again.

For example, you set up a plan with Vanguard and pay the 0.3% that year. Before the annual fee kicks in for the second year, drop the program and rebalance the account yourself.

Five years later, you retire and aren't sure how to best set up your accounts in retirement. Use their service again, paying the 0.3% fee for as long as you need it. In the meantime, you've saved several years worth of fees.

It may not sound like much but if you save even 1% on a $500,000 account over several years, that's an extra $5,000 per year in your pocket.

Robo-Advisors

Robo-advisors are becoming more popular. They are computer programs that choose your investments for you based on complex algorithms that take risk and growth into account.

You can choose portfolios that are conservative, aggressive, income oriented, growth oriented, and so on. These robo-advisors mostly use ETFs as the investment vehicles.

Wealthfront and Betterment are two of the largest and most well-known robo-advisors. They typically charge about 0.25% to start. But as the name suggests, you'll have very little interaction with a human. If you want to talk with someone about your account, you'll usually have to pay a little more. It's still cheaper than a full service advisor, but not as inexpensive as Vanguard or something similar.

The nice thing about robo-advisors is they usually have very low or no minimum account sizes. With Vanguard, Schwab, and the like you typically need about $50,000 for portfolio management, though it will vary from broker to broker.

Pay Nothing

There are a few brokers out there now where you will pay nothing for transaction costs or annual fees. You won't get any advice. But you won't pay anything when you trade.

Well, not exactly.

These companies, like Robin Hood, aren't charities. They haven't been set up out of the good will of their founders' hearts to bleed money so that investors don't pay commissions.

They are keeping the lights on somehow. So even if you're not paying a commission or fee, they are making money from you.

The companies earn interest on the cash sitting in your account, lend it out, collect interest, and likely get paid for order flow.

In other words, when you place a trade, rather than send your order to the exchange that will get you the best price, it may send your order somewhere else to get executed because they're getting paid to do so. As a result, you may buy the stock for a penny per share more.

If you're buying 500 shares of stock, that costs you $5. So even though you didn't pay a commission, you paid $5 extra for your transaction.

There's no such thing as a free lunch – particularly on Wall Street. Remember, if you're getting something for free, it's not really free.

Index Funds

There is almost never a reason to pay for an actively managed mutual fund.

An actively managed fund is where a fund manager picks the stocks that go into the portfolio. If he thinks Apple is a good buy, he'll add shares. Some managers will add stocks because they are in a sector or geographical region that they think will do well.

Whatever the reason is, a human being makes the decision when to buy and when to sell stocks in the portfolio.

The problem is most human beings are bad investors – even professionals who went to Ivy League schools.

In 2016, only 40% of actively managed mutual funds outperformed their benchmarks (such as the S&P 500). So the majority didn't.

The numbers get abysmal once you go out more than one year. From 2014 to 2016 only 8% outperformed.

In other words over three years, more than nine out of 10 actively managed mutual funds underperformed their benchmarks.[1]

To make matters worse, you pay for that weak performance.

The average expense ratio for an actively managed large cap mutual fund is 1.25%.[2]

That means your manager has to beat the market by 1.25% just to break even with the overall market.

If the market generates an 8.75% return, the fund needs a gain of 10% just to match the market's performance.

That's not easy to do. And as I showed you, the overwhelming majority of fund managers can't.

By the way, those expense ratios go up once you get into mid caps, small caps, foreign stocks, sector specific funds, and so on.

There is a strong inverse correlation between investment returns and cost. The more you pay, the worse your returns are. If you're paying a 5% load (fee) just to get into a fund, plus a 1.25% expense ratio, there is no way you are going to beat the market, unless you're incredibly lucky.

Besides owning Perpetual Dividend Raisers for the long term, the most cost-effective way to invest (and increase your returns) is to buy and hold index funds.

Index funds are mutual funds that follow an index, such as the S&P 500 or the Russell 2000. It can even be region-specific like Asia, country-specific like Canada, or sector-specific such as biotech.

Index funds typically have expense ratios of 0.2% or lower, though some of the very specialized and foreign indexes may have slightly higher expense ratios.

Index funds are cheaper because the fund companies don't have to pay for managers, analysts, and research trips like an actively managed fund company.

---

[1] http://www.thinkadvisor.com/2017/04/12/think-longevity-not-just-performance-when-buying-a.

[2] https://www.thebalance.com/average-expense-ratios-for-mutual-funds-2466612.

An index fund manager simply has to ensure his or her fund is following the index.

It doesn't matter if the fund manager thinks Apple is a screaming buy. If Apple makes up 2% of the index, then Apple will make up 2% of the fund.

If the fund manager has a bad feeling about the market, he or she can't just start selling and go to cash. The money must stay invested in the stocks that make up the index.

And considering how wrong these fund managers are, that's a good thing.

The Vanguard 500 Index Fund (VFINX), one of the larger index funds around with $310 billion in assets, has an expense ratio of just 0.14%.[3]

Compare that to the Fidelity Contrafund (FCNTX), an actively managed large cap stock fund. Contrafund has a reasonable expense ratio of 0.68%.[4] Over five years, it's annual performance trailed the S&P 500 by 0.7% – almost exactly its expense ratio.

Contrafund investors made less money than if they invested in an index fund. The difference between what they made and could have made was paid directly to Fidelity.

Why would you ever pay for an actively managed fund when the odds are that you won't make as much money as you would in an index fund?

Take the money you'll save and go to Vegas instead. At least there you have a shot at a big payoff.

In Vegas the odds are slightly worse than 50-50, but if you win you'll double your money. With an actively managed mutual fund your odds are worse than at the blackjack table. And if you win, you might make three or four percentage points more than you would have in an index fund.

I will say this again: Working with an investment professional can be incredibly helpful, particularly if you're not comfortable handling your investments yourself.

If you need guidance on retirement planning, insurance products, estate planning, or are just less stressed knowing that someone is watching your portfolio and will make the necessary adjustments for you – a good investment professional is worth paying for.

---

[3]https://www.thebalance.com/average-expense-ratios-for-mutual-funds-2466612.

[4]https://www.morningstar.com/funds/xnas/fcntx/quote.html.

But if you don't need those services, or only need them once, use the lowest cost methods of investing to keep more money in your pocket.

Better yet, let the money in your portfolio compound or generate income. Every dollar that you're paying a stockbroker or a mutual fund company is a dollar that is not working for you.

Keep your costs low.

Actions to Take

- Stop losing 1% of your assets every year to an advisor if you don't need the help.
- If you do need asset allocation help, save money by using advisors at Vanguard, Schwab, or other discount brokers and mutual fund companies.
- Buying Perpetual Dividend Raisers and holding them for the long term is one of the least expensive strategies available.
- There's no free lunch on Wall Street. If you're getting something for free, check your pockets. They're getting picked somehow.

CHAPTER 13

How to Buy a Car for 25% Off

"When my car runs out of gas, I buy a new one. I don't want to ride around in a quitter."

– Stephen Colbert

I've bought one new car in my life. And it was exciting. As gas prices were soaring 10 years ago, I waited three weeks for a brand spanking new Toyota Prius.

At the time, Priuses were in high demand. Gas prices had gone over $3 per gallon for the first time, and a lot of people were attracted to the gas efficiency of the hybrid autos.

I loved that car. I averaged 50 miles per gallon and, before it hit 100,000 miles, traded it in. Only this time, when I bought a car, I got it for 25% less than the Prius.

And the car after that was a higher-end model.

How did I do it?

I bought used.

Now before you think I bought an old clunker, that's not how I roll.

You can get a nearly brand new car, but for far less than you'd pay for a new one.

In fact, the minute a new car drives off the lot, it is worth 20% to 30% less than it was 60 seconds earlier.

So I let the little old lady who only drove to church on Sundays take the depreciation. And then I buy the car after she's owned it for a couple of months.

When I buy a used car, I typically get it with less than 20,000 miles and preferably fewer than 10,000. My current car only had 7,500 miles on it when I bought it.

So what do prices look like in the real world?

As I write this, in South Florida you can buy a 2016 used Lexus ES 350 Premium with 11,000 miles for a listed price of $36,991. But you can probably get it cheaper. The average certified pre-owned price at a dealer in South Florida is $35,498, according to Kelly Blue Book.

Also according to Kelley Blue Book, a 2017 new Lexus ES 350 has a fair purchase price of $39,847.

So you can save nearly $4,500 by choosing the car with 11,000 miles on it.

The fair purchase price for a new 2017 Ford Explorer base model is $30,987. Buy it certified pre-owned from a dealer with 20,000 miles on it, and it costs you $26,354. If the car is bought from a dealer but not certified pre-owned, you can save another $800. And if you buy it from a private party, the savings are significant. The same car will only be $22,499.

With only 10,000 miles, the price only goes up about $800.

When it comes to used cars, I only buy certified pre-owned. I pay more than if I bought it off a guy on Craigslist or Autotrader, but the certification is worth it to me.

Certified pre-owned means the cars are in good shape, often have low mileage, have been inspected by the dealer, and usually still have the manufacturer's warranty.

Even though the car I'm buying has low mileage and has likely been owned for less than a year, I assume it wasn't driven by the little old lady only on her way to church on Sundays.

So I feel better knowing that the car has been thoroughly examined and that the dealer will stand by the car if something goes wrong. And of course, the manufacturer's warranty is critical.

You can save money if you buy it direct from the seller, rather than through a dealership. Keep in mind, you'll have fewer protections and recourse if something goes wrong.

If you're a car person and know how to inspect and fix one, you can save thousands buying directly from the seller. And that way, you'll get an idea of just how little the seller is like a little old lady.

How Much Should You Pay?

Fortunately, there are great free resources on the web that can help you determine a fair price for a car that you're interested in.

Kelley Blue Book is considered the authority on used car values. Its website, www.kbb.com, is free.

On their site, you can enter a wide range of variables besides the model of the car and mileage. For example, the region of the country where you buy your car will have an effect on the price.

A 2016 Hyundai Elantra GT with 18,000 miles has a fair value of $14,782 if you buy it certified pre-owned in my zip code in South Florida.

In the suburbs of New York City, it will cost you about $120 more.

The same car in San Francisco is $15,462.

If you're in San Francisco, it probably doesn't make sense to buy the car in Florida and drive it or ship it in order to save $700. But you should be aware of some regional differences in price.

Now that you know the fair value of the car, it's time for everyone's least favorite thing – haggling with the salesperson.

Have the maximum price you are willing to pay in mind. After that you MUST be willing to walk away. Even if you've been there all day – which is a tactic the dealer will use. If you've been there for hours, they know you don't want to have to start the process all over again.

A few years ago, I was car shopping with my wife and kids. I took the car I wanted out for a test drive, and we started the negotiations. The dealer started with a ridiculous number.

We played the game. I countered, she'd check with her manager and would come back with a slightly lower price. I'd counter again, a few bucks higher than my original offer. This went on for a while, and we weren't getting close.

I pulled out my checkbook and told her the maximum I'd be willing to pay. "I'll write the check right now if we have a deal. Otherwise, I'm leaving," I said.

She looked at my kids, who were getting fidgety and responded, "I know you don't want to drag those kids to another dealer, so let's just get this done." And then she gave me a higher price than the one I stated.

I told her I'd given her my maximum price and that she was about to lose a sale. She, of course, had to talk to her manager. I gave her five minutes. While she was still in there with the manager, probably talking about something besides my offer, I had my wife and kids put their coats on. She came rushing out and told me she couldn't come down in price any further.

I thanked her for her time and walked out.

The next day, she called and asked if I was still interested in the car. I wasn't.

I'd found what I was looking for somewhere else. It was the same car and price as she was offering me but with less mileage on the vehicle.

Be ready, willing, and able to walk away.

Another tactic is to get the price of the car before you commit to a trade-in. Dealers know that you'll likely have a trade-in and will package it together. It's certainly easier but you may not always get the best deal.

There are some businesses that set up near car dealers that offer trade-in services. They don't sell cars to the public. They only buy them. They often advertise that you'll get as much as 10% more than at the dealer for your trade-in.

Definitely check them out if they're available. Get the offer in writing. In fact, you should try to get a few offers in writing so that if you are going to trade in your car when you buy the next one, you'll know what the fair price is for your old car.

When the salesperson asks you if you'll be trading in your car as part of your purchase, you can tell them you're not sure and you won't be lying. Say, "Let's focus on buying the car and if we have a deal, we can talk about the trade-in."

That way, you can be sure you're getting the best deal on just the car you're buying. After that, you can negotiate for your trade-in.

If you hate negotiating, CarMax has a no-haggling policy. The price of the car on the lot is the price you'll pay. You may not get a great deal, but the experience is more pleasant.

The salespeople are paid a flat fee per transaction. It doesn't matter if you buy a 1980 Dodge Dart with 350,000 miles on it or a 2017 Porsche 911 Turbo with 1,200 miles on it. The salesperson will receive the same commission. So he or she is incented to make sure you're happy with your purchase.

They receive bonuses for selling things like warranties and other products or services. As for the car itself, they have no motivation to put you into a more expensive car than you're looking for.

In my experience, CarMax's prices are fair – but like I said, you won't find a bargain. Carmax's network also allows you to get the exact car you want even if it's located in another part of the country. They'll ship it to your closest CarMax dealership, usually for a fee of several hundred dollars.

You can also check out eBay Motors.

It may feel strange buying a car online, particularly through a site known for auctions of collectibles and knick-knacks, but you can sometimes find good values there.

You should always be sure of whom you're dealing with (a dealer, a private party, etc.) and understand the terms. (Can you return the car if you're not happy?)

eBay offers a Vehicle Purchase Protection plan that covers the buyer in the case of fraud, liens, undisclosed damage, and more.

If you're comfortable with this kind of transaction, eBay can save you a lot of money.

Timing Is Everything

Well, maybe not everything, but you might be able to take advantage of a salesperson's desperation to make quota. And what's more fun than seeing a used car salesperson sweat?

Most salespeople have quotas. They must sell a certain number of cars by a certain period – usually the end of the month. If they hit that quota, they may be eligible for bonuses for each car they sell above the quota.

So at the end of the month, you may have a very motivated sales-person – and their manager. If it's been a bad month, they may do whatever it takes to get you to sign the papers. As a result, you may be able to dictate terms in a way you wouldn't the week before.

On the flip side, if the salesperson is having a good month, taking a few dollars off the price may not be a big deal because they may be getting a larger commission on each car they sell.

I once had the good fortune of seeing the sales tally for all of the salespeople at the dealership while I was negotiating. My salesperson was not having a good month, so I negotiated hard, knowing they were desperate.

"I don't need to buy a car today," I said. "But I know you need to sell one."

No doubt, buying a new car is fun and exciting. And who doesn't love that new car smell? Everyone should experience buying a new car once in his or her life. There is a certain pride that comes with that first new car.

But after that initial experience, you're better off buying a slightly used car. You'll save a ton of money and someone else will eat the $5,000 or so in depreciation for driving it off the lot.

Actions to Take

- Buy used with low mileage instead of new. You'll save thousands of dollars.
- Use the free information on the web to know how much you should be paying for the car you want in your part of the country.
- When negotiating, be prepared to walk out.
- Make the salesperson squirm. It's so much fun.

CHAPTER 14

How to Travel for Less

"Airplane travel is nature's way of making you look like your passport photo."

– Al Gore

When I think back on my favorite memories of the past 20 years, many of them involve family trips.

Our dream vacation to Italy, an Australian and Indonesian cruise, visits to my brother in Los Angeles, and many more.

For me (and many people) travel is one of the most fun and exciting parts of life. Seeing historical sites, eating local cuisine, meeting new people from different cultures – it's the best. Just thinking about it now makes me eager to get back on the road.

Travel, particularly to foreign countries, can be expensive, even when the cost of living in those countries is low. The price of airline tickets is only going up, and there seem to be few bargains at nice hotels.

This chapter won't tell you to stay in cheap motels or hostels to save money. If you want to do that, by all means, go for it. It will save you a lot of dough. I did that many times when I was younger. But now that I'm older, I like to stay in nicer places. It doesn't have to be a five-star resort, but a clean hotel with various amenities is a must.

What I will show you in this chapter is how to travel at the level you'd like for less.

Airline Affinity Cards

We're all bombarded by credit card offers. But some of them are more useful than others.

If you know where you want to travel, figure out which airlines offer the best routes and fares to get there. Then take a look at their credit cards.

Most airlines offer credit cards that come with generous bonuses to sign up, plus extra bonuses once you spend a certain amount in the first few months.

For example, when we were planning a trip to Italy a few years ago, American Airlines was our best option.

My wife and I signed up separately for the American Airlines Mastercard. At the time, we each received 50,000 miles, plus another 10,000 once we spent $3,000 in the first three months.

We charged everything on those cards for the next three months to get the bonus, along with the other miles that come with spending. It didn't matter if I was buying a $2 item at CVS; it went on the card.

Most airlines allow you to combine miles among family members, so by the time we were ready to book, we had a free ticket.

Occasionally, some incredible deal will pop up for a very limited time. A friend of ours got the same card but with a 100,000-mile bonus. That offer was gone by the time we signed up.

If you're traveling with another family member, make sure you get separate cards, not cards that are linked to each other. Fill out individual applications. That way you'll both get whatever bonus is being offered.

This should probably go without saying, but you need to pay the entire balance of these cards every month. It makes no sense to get airline miles but pay 15% interest on your purchases. You'll end up paying more than you'll save.

And assuming you'll pay the balance every month, use those cards for everything – groceries; everyday expenses; heck, even big-ticket items like a car. Most dealers will allow you to charge a few thousand dollars on your card. So if you were going to write a check, you may as well put $3,000 on your card and get those miles.

There are many sources to see which cards have the best offers. Most of the major financial magazines and websites publish articles comparing the various cards.

ThePointsGuy.com is a free site that regularly updates its comparisons on cards. It also publishes some amazing airfare deals.

TheSimpleDollar.com is another site that compares credit card offers. If you're doing other travel, such as to visit the grandkids or for work, try to stick with the same airline. If you get up to one of their elite statuses, you get bonus miles when you travel.

Airline credit cards are great ways to cut the cost of air travel.

Eat, Drink, and Get Miles

Additionally, some airlines and hotels have dining rewards programs. You just go to a restaurant that is affiliated with the program and receive miles or points based on how much you spend.

You have to register your credit card with the rewards program, and you'll only get points if you use that card. So if you use a different one or pay cash, the program will have no idea that you ate at a participating restaurant. Note that you usually can register any credit card with the program, not just an affinity card for that airline or hotel.

You may find that the hottest restaurants are not part of the program – basically because they don't need to be. But there are plenty of restaurants that do participate in the hopes of attracting diners who want to rack up points.

What I like about the program is that it's automatic. You get points just by using the card. I don't go out of my way to find restaurants that are in the program (though I'm sure people do). But if I happen to eat at a participating restaurant, I get points.

Recently, I traveled to New York City and met friends at a popular tapas restaurant. My bill was $157. I didn't check to see if the place was part of the American Airlines Dining Rewards program, which is the one I'm in. I didn't even think about it.

But I just noticed that I received 471 miles for that visit. I collected 3 miles per dollar spent. Now, 471 miles won't exactly get me to Europe, but 471 miles here, 50 miles for picking up a sandwich at the deli near my office, 100 miles for a quick bite out, and it starts to add up.

Most of the big airlines have dining rewards programs. Hilton also has one.

Now, don't think you'll be slick and enroll in all of them and collect points on every airline whenever you eat out. They're on to you. If you enroll in more than one dining rewards program, only the one that you signed up for last will be active.

Since you're already spending the money at these restaurants and the programs are free to join, you'd be crazy not to. You simply get miles or points for doing what you would have done anyway.

Don't Stay at a Hotel

I like hotels.

I like using the fitness center, grabbing a drink at the bar, getting help from the concierge or the front desk, and so on.

But in some cities they are very expensive. Try staying in New York City or San Francisco for less than $250 a night. You'll be sleeping on a cardboard box on the sidewalk.

Over the past few years, short-term apartment and house rentals have become very popular. Sites like Airbnb, VRBO, and Homeaway allow travelers to rent apartments and houses for far less than you could stay in a hotel.

Of course, the apartment or house won't come with the amenities you get in a hotel, but there are other benefits besides the cheaper price. You can get some excellent recommendations from the owner on places to go from a local's perspective. You can also cook some meals rather than going out if you want to save money that way.

The booking process is just like booking a hotel online. You go to one of the sites, find a place you want to rent, and if it's available, book it.

One thing you definitely want to do is check out the reviews. You'd like to see a listing that has lots of positive reviews. If the owner is brand new to the site, you have no idea if they are legitimate, easy to work with, or if the place is as advertised.

They could very well be a great person with a beautiful property. But unless there are lots of reviews, they are a wild card. Everyone has to get his or her start somewhere, but it's not going to be with me. And it shouldn't be with you either.

You can usually communicate with the owner before booking to ask questions. Their responsiveness is a good indicator of how your transaction will go. If someone doesn't get back to you quickly, don't bother with them.

Read the reviews carefully. See how easy the check-in process was. It's not like a hotel where there's a front desk. Often the person just meets you with the key or even leaves it somewhere.

You want to see a history of hassle-free check-ins. The last thing you want is to be in a strange city or country and not be able to get into your place or have to scramble to find somewhere to stay because you can't get in.

In 2015, I traveled to Italy with my wife and two kids. We were originally booked in two rooms in a hotel that were each more than $400 a night for three days. Rome is expensive. We were there during tourist season so it was tough to find a decent hotel for less.

We found an apartment on Airbnb instead. It was a studio apartment with a loft and pull-out couch. My wife and I stayed in the loft and my kids on the pull-out couch. It was in a nondescript building with a five-minute walk to the Coliseum.

To be honest, the apartment was nothing special. It was clean and a little cramped, but it cost $275 a night rather than $800 for two hotel rooms.

The owner lived in the apartment next door with her family. We never met her but communicated via text. We asked her for restaurant suggestions but said we didn't want a tourist trap. We wanted to know where she goes with her family.

She recommended a tiny place that has continuously been occupied by a restaurant since the 1500s. There was no English on the menu, and the waiter had to interpret everything for us. No one spoke English at the tables around us.

It was the best meal we had in Italy, which is saying a lot.

And because we weren't staying at a hotel in a major tourist center – we were in a residential neighborhood, we frequented other local places that don't appear in any guidebook.

Lastly, being in an apartment with a kitchen allowed us to buy some groceries. So we didn't have to eat breakfast out, saving some money.

We had another terrific experience in Ashland, Oregon.

We stayed in someone's in-law unit attached to their house. We had our own entrance and kitchen. We never had to see the owner if we didn't want to.

It turns out he was a very nice guy, who had a chicken coop in the back and let our kids feed the chickens. More importantly, he told us about a beautiful lake that was a 10-minute walk from his house.

We had done our homework on the area and had read about the lake, but it didn't pique our interest. He insisted we check it out. We ended up spending the whole day there. It was wonderful.

Concierges and front desk people never give you that local flavor, even when you ask them for it. I've only had those experiences with Airbnb and the like.

Read those reviews. *Any* red flags, move on to the next one. Not everyone is going to have the perfect experience, but if you read anything that sounds strange or makes you uncomfortable, don't stay there.

Unless you're somewhere fairly rural, there should be plenty of properties to choose from.

Free Walking Tours

If you're visiting a city and have the stamina, consider a free walking tour rather than paying for an expensive tour. Besides saving money, you'll work up an appetite for lunch or dinner. And you'll have a better appreciation of the places you're seeing, rather than jumping off a bus, snapping a photo, and getting back on the bus.

Go online and do a search for "free walking tour (city name)" or look for them on Tripadvisor.com. There will usually be reviews and ratings of the tour company and/or guide, especially on Tripadvisor.

Not all of the guides are licensed or registered. In cities where that's required, they are licensed. But a license is not needed in all cities.

With some tours, you have to sign up in advance. With others you don't. If you have to sign up, make sure you do. These tours are often very popular and will sell out.

You will meet the tour at a designated time and place. A few minutes later you're on your way. Normally, you don't have much time to shop or eat. It's a cursory tour of the city or certain neighborhoods. They typically last about two hours, maybe three. The guides are usually very knowledgeable and often quite entertaining.

They are billed as free, but don't be a cheapskate. The only way the guides make money is from tips, so you should tip what you feel the tour was worth. As I said, they are usually very good. Depending on the tour, I tend to tip $10 to $20 per person.

Read the reviews online so you can be confident you're getting a good tour. Reviews will often point out highlights and any unusual information that you may need. And if you're inclined, post a review after you're done to help others.

The nice thing about these tours is that if you see something you want to explore, you can hop off the tour at anytime. There's no count to make sure you're on the bus.

I've had several memorable free walking tours. In Portland, Oregon, our guide had a monopoly on the free walking tour business. It wasn't hard to see why. He was a stand-up comedian who gave tours during the day. Not only was he hysterical, he knew the city very well and took us to places we wouldn't have found on our own.

In Venice, Italy, we hooked up with a company that gives walking tours. The tour guide was a college student who grew up in Venice spoke perfect English, and was terrific, answering every question my children (11 and 14 years old) threw at her.

These free walking tours have become quite popular and are available in many cities, so go online and check it out the next time you're traveling.

Cruise for Free (or Close to It)

If you're comfortable talking in front of a crowd, you may be able to cruise for free.

Cruise lines are always looking for speakers for their enrichment programs. You should have a specialty and a passion for your subject matter. And you need to be entertaining. You can't get away with giving a dry lecture on the Peloponnesian War.

Whatever your expertise, you need to make it come to life.

Cruise lines bring on guest lecturers for a wide variety of topics including politics/current events, history, entertainment, sciences, and so on.

You can try to track down the enrichment director of a cruise line, but your best bet is to get placed by an agency that specializes in cruise lecturers.

Some of the well-known ones are Sixth Star Entertainment and Marketing, Posh Talks, Tim Castle, To Sea with Z, The Working Vacation, and Compass Speakers and Entertainment.

Look up their websites for how to contact them.

You don't have to pay to apply to be a lecturer. If any agency asks for money up front, don't walk away – run. They are a scam.

Reputable agencies may charge you a fee of $50 to $100 per day that you are on the cruise, but only if you are placed. You will also likely be responsible for tips, travel to the port, and your bar bill.

Every cruise line and placement agency is different, so be sure you understand all of the details and what you are responsible for before boarding the ship.

Gentlemen Hosts

Usually, it's the women who get free stuff. (When was the last time you were offered free drinks at the bar on Men's Night?) But distinguished gentlemen can cruise for free, provided they know how to dance.

Many cruise lines bring on board men ages 40 to 70 who will dance with the single women. You'll be working hard as it's your job to ensure that the women are having fun and feel special and that everyone who wants to gets to dance the night away.

But before you get any ideas, sexual relationships are typically discouraged or prohibited by the cruise line.

Besides being a good dancer, you should be very social. Not only will you be doing the fox trot in the evenings, you may be expected to participate in other activities such as touring, games, and dining.

In return for your charms, gentlemen hosts receive a free cabin, dining room privileges, beverage and laundry allowances, on shore excursions, and other perks.

Many of the agencies that book guest lecturers also place gentlemen hosts.

So if you're single, sociable, and well mannered, brush up on your rumba and start cruising for free.

Having the free time to travel is one of the great benefits of retirement. You can make it less costly with these pointers so that you can afford longer or more frequent trips.

Actions to Take

- Choose your next credit card by where and how you want to travel.
- Enroll in dining rewards programs. They're free.
- Take free walking tours.
- If you're traveling to Ashland, Oregon, I can recommend a nice place with a great chicken coop.

PART

III

Small Ideas That Add Up

"Great things are done by a series of small things brought together."

– Vincent Van Gogh

In this section, I'll show you ideas that can save you money or return cash to your pocket.

Each strategy likely won't mean thousands of extra dollars for you. But if you use them together, they very well could.

Best of all, they are simple to use.

Like all of the methods in this book, you don't have to go through complicated steps or learn complex skills to use them. Usually, it's a few extra mouse clicks in addition to what you were already doing, but it means instant savings or cold hard cash returned to you.

Lastly, many of them are fun. Taking classes, listening to music, and getting cash for unwanted stuff aren't exactly going down into the salt mines all day. These strategies can be used by anyone, but are especially good for someone who is already retired.

Just using one of these strategies likely covers the cost of this book. Two of them and you've paid for the several copies you bought for your friends and family.

If you have any cool strategies you'd like to share, email me at feedback@uberretirementbook.com.

15

Small Ideas That Add Up

"Notice the small things. The rewards are inversely proportional."

– Liz Vassey

Reward Sites

If you shop online, you're leaving money on the table unless you use the various cash back and reward sites that are out there.

These sites offer cash or points that can be used for gift cards, cash, or merchandise. They are typically free and simple to use. All you do is create an account and when you want to shop at your favorite online store, sign in and search for the merchant that you're interested in.

Once you find it, click on it and you're taken to the merchant's site. The prices and offerings are the same as if you went direct. The only difference is you'll get cash back or points for your purchases.

Let's take a look at a few of the popular ones and how they work.

eBates

eBates (www.ebates.com) is probably my favorite because you receive a check every three months, as long as you have earned $5.01 or more in cash back.

When you shop using eBates, you'll get anywhere from 1% to 40% back in cash. Now, before you get too excited, I've never seen anything close to 40%, but that's what they say is possible.

The highest I've seen on anything I've ordered is 10%. But whatever the amount is, it's free money. You're getting a percentage of your purchases back in cold hard cash every three months.

You can even earn cash back from in-store purchases if you link your credit card to your account and click on an offer before you go to the store. You can also do it on your phone once you're in the store if it's an impromptu shopping trip.

I would strongly caution not to add credit card information to your account when you're in a store using an unsecure Wi-Fi network or cellular data. Get your account set up with your credit card when you're home. Then, you can check eBates when you're in a store and click on an offer. Once you do, you're all set to receive cash back as long as you use the linked credit card.

Or do what I do and click on all offers that you may use at some point, so you don't have to think about it when you're at the store. I'm not in Bed Bath & Beyond very often. And if I am, I'm sure I'd forget to check eBates. So I just linked it ahead of time so that if I'm ever there, I'm sure to get my 4% back – just for doing my normal shopping.

eBates has a wide range of stores that you can use, many of them household names, and some of them will be new stores you never heard of.

For example, as I write this (the deals change from time to time), you can get 14% back when you shop at Barnes & Noble, 6% from JC Penney, and 6% from Macy's.

I especially like finding stores that I'm unfamiliar with when buying gifts for people. You come across some unique stores and products.

eBates also has deals from time to time so you may get discounts on whatever you buy. Chances are, you can find similar discounts elsewhere online, but at least here you'll get the cash back on top of whatever discount is being offered.

eBates has been around since 1998, so they have a long track record in business. I've used it for about 10 years and never had a problem with them.

If I'm shopping online, I go to eBates first. One extra click gets me a check every three months, so there's really no reason not to do it.

MyPoints

MyPoints (www.mypoints.com) works in a similar fashion. You visit the MyPoints website and simply click through to your favorite stores (or new stores). Instead of receiving cash back, you'll accumulate points that can be exchanged for gift cards and other items.

With MyPoints you can also earn points by watching videos, printing and redeeming coupons, taking surveys, or clicking on ads that are sent to your email inbox.

You won't earn a ton of points with those methods. You really need to buy stuff using MyPoints to accumulate a meaningful amount. But if you answer enough surveys, click on enough ads, or watch enough videos, it can certainly add to your stash of points.

When you shop, you earn points per dollar spent. Stores all have different deals. For example, if you shop on HSN.com, you earn eight points per dollar. Banana Republic offers four points per dollar.

There are also special offers like 1,000 points with a purchase of $30 or more at Swap.com, 1,500 points for subscribing to the *Wall Street Journal,* or 2,850 points when you sign a new contract with Verizon Wireless.

Keep in mind that offers change all the time, so the deals that I mentioned here may be different by the time you read this.

Once you have earned enough points, you can redeem them for gift cards.

Gift cards start as low as $5, but the point totals you need depend on the merchant.

For example, you need 1,590 points for a $10 Walmart gift card but only 1,410 points for a $10 AMC Theaters gift card.

Currently, MyPoints offers gift cards from 70 businesses including American Airlines, Amazon.com, and Red Robin Gourmet Burgers.

To get the most out of MyPoints you have to game the system a bit. As I mentioned, there is a difference in required point totals for each company. So if you're a customer of both Walmart and AMC Theaters, you're better off getting the AMC Theaters $10 gift card and saving yourself 180 points.

You'll want to look at the various cards and point totals to see which ones you'd use and what the best deal is at the time.

And like everything else on these sites, things change often.

You can also earn more points by installing the MyPoints toolbar on your computer. That way when you shop, you don't take the extra step and have to visit the webpage and click through.

Personally, I don't like to install software like that on my computer. I'm sure I've missed out on lots of points, but it's one less entity tracking my every move online.

Usually, gift cards are excluded from earning points on MyPoints, but if you buy them on MyGiftCardsPlus.com and link your MyPoints account, you will earn points on gift card purchases.

For more information on how to get gift cards at a discount, read the next section.

MyPoints is owned by Prodege, which has been in business since 2005.

Swagbucks

Prodege also owns Swagbucks (www.swagbucks.com). The program appears to be very similar to MyPoints with many of the same partners.

You either go to the site to click through to a store or install the toolbar. Then, when you shop, you earn points that can be redeemed for gift cards.

Just like MyPoints, you can also earn points by watching videos, answering surveys, and other methods.

Since I have a MyPoints account, I don't see a need for Swagbucks. But if you don't belong to one of the programs, you can sign up for either. I just wouldn't do both as that's one more account to have to keep track of. You might as well keep all of your points in one place.

Upromise

Upromise (www.upromise.com) is a different concept. Similar to the others, you visit their site and click through to online stores to earn rewards. But in Upromise's case, the rewards are contributions to a college savings account.

You can choose a 529 plan offered by Upromise or can link to many others.

I have a 529 plan for one of my kids that is run by a large brokerage house. I was able to link my Upromise account to it and whenever I have $25 or more in rewards, the funds are automatically deposited in the account.

You can also sign up for Upromise Dining. Once you link your credit cards to your account, any time you eat at a participating restaurant, you earn 2.5% of your bill for your account. It's similar to the airline and hotel dining rewards mentioned earlier in the book.

If you spend $100 at the restaurant (not including tax and tip), your account will be credited $2.50.

You don't have to do anything when you go to the restaurant – simply pay with a linked credit card. Upromise has a list of restaurants on its site that are part of the program.

Upromise offers a Mastercard that allows you to earn cash for college on every purchase, not only the vendors that are partners with Upromise.

You can also accelerate your earnings by linking family members to your account.

While all of these reward programs will give you some kind of bonus for referring friends or family, Upromise will deposit money in your account if your friends or family are linked to it.

For example, if you have a child going to college in a few years, you could set the grandparents up with an Upromise account and every time they buy something, going through the Upromise site first, the cash will be deposited in your child's account.

The same goes if you're the grandparent. Set up the account to help out your grandchild and tell your kids to do their online shopping through Upromise to multiply the earnings.

Upromise also has a small list of local retailers that participate in the program. Again, you can earn rewards if you shop in the store with your registered card.

Like the other programs, Upromise offers rewards on a wide variety of retailers and vendors.

You can earn 5% on Mac Cosmetics, 5% on Office Depot, and 3% on a Walt Disney World vacation package. If you're going to Disney World, chances are you're going to spend a few thousand dollars. Three percent adds up quickly.

Cash is deposited in the 529 account quarterly, once a minimum has been hit. The minimum depends on the specific 529 plan, but most of them require a minimum of $25 for a deposit to be made.

So if you only have $20 this quarter, you'll have to wait until you earn another $5. If you earn $10 the next quarter, you'll receive the full $30 at the end of that quarter.

Earning cash back from online shopping couldn't be easier. Once you're registered with the sites, just go there first and click on the link to the retailer where you're shopping.

Whether it's air travel, sporting goods, clothes, or any of the many other things you shop for, using these sites can put hundreds or even thousands of dollars back in your pocket.

Buy and Sell Gift Cards

We've all received gift cards that we'll never use. They get put in a drawer somewhere and sit there until we move and have to clean out all of our junk drawers.

Or, if you're like me, you move the junk drawer with you.

I have a Foot Locker gift card from 2012 still sitting in a drawer. And a frozen yogurt gift card from three years ago that I've never used. And I like frozen yogurt. I'm just not near that particular place that often, so I don't keep the card in my wallet.

So it sits unused.

Fortunately, there are sites for people like me.

On these websites you can buy and sell gift cards – for less than face value. As a buyer, you get a discount – often a meaningful one. As a seller, you won't get the full value for you card, but it's found cash when you consider you're not going to use the card anyway.

And buyers of gift cards can do their regular shopping at significant discounts.

For example, you can get Walgreen's gift cards at a 10% discount to their value. So it's like getting 10% off when you walk into the store.

You can get an 11% discount at Pizza Hut and 18% off at 1-800-Flowers. Keep in mind, these aren't discounts to the prices at the store or coupons. These are gift cards that are used like cash. So if you have other discounts or coupons that lower the price, you use your $50 gift card that you paid $45 for and you're getting another 10% off the price you paid.

It's a terrific deal. I'm surprised more people don't go to these sites and buy cards, just to save some money. Not all the discounts are that large. Some are only a few percentage points. But better that money stay in your pocket than in a retailer's.

Below, I'll review three of the top card swapping sites.

In addition, I'll compare the sites to see how much I'd get for my $50 Foot Locker gift card and how much I'd pay for a $50 Lowe's card.

Cardpool

Cardpool (www.cardpool.com) will pay up to 92% of the value of your card. You can opt to receive cash or payment in the form of an Amazon.com gift card. You'll receive 6% more if you take the Amazon card than if you want cash.

The Amazon card is electronic and will be emailed to you within one business day. Physical checks typically take 5 to 10 business days.

If you have a physical card, Cardpool will send you a mailing label to ship the card to them. You can also sell back electronic gift cards. You just have to provide the code to Cardpool so they can verify the total remaining on the card.

To sell a card on Cardpool, it must have a value of at least $25. There cannot be any restrictions or expiration date on the card.

You can sell the card even if you've used some of it. If the card was originally $50 and you've spent $13.11, you can sell the remaining $36.89. As along as it has a remaining value of $25 or more, Cardpool will accept it.

Cardpool also has physical kiosks and cashiers around the country in places like Safeway, Stop & Shop, and Ace Cash Express.

If you don't like the price Cardpool is offering, you can list it in on their marketplace where you may get more, though there's no guarantee your card will sell. If you sell it directly to Cardpool, the transaction will be done quickly. Listing it on their marketplace may take a while, or you may never get your requested price.

There are no fees to buy or sell cards on Cardpool.

Amount offered for $50 Foot Locker card: $38.95 (Amazon gift card) or $36.75 in cash

Discount on Best Buy card: 3%

GiftCardBin

Giftcardbin (www.giftcardbin.com) will pay up to 93% of the value of your card. The cards must have a minimum value of $10. They also can have expiration dates, though don't expect to get top price for a card that will expire soon.

Like Cardpool, Giftcardbin accepts electronic gift cards and has physical locations (typically at check cashing stores) in addition to its website.

When you sell a card, you can get paid with a check or electronically through PayPal.

There are no fees to buy or sell cards on GiftCardBin.

Amount offered for $50 Foot Locker card: $34

Discount on Best Buy Card: 3%

Raise

Raise (www.raise.com) is a bit different than the other sites. Whereas the other sites directly buy the card from you and then sell it to the buyer, keeping the difference, Raise is more of a marketplace to connect buyers and sellers.

As the seller, you determine the price you're willing to accept for your card. Raise will then take a 12% commission for facilitating the transaction. As a seller, you'll also pay the greater of $1 or 1% to sell a physical card. That fee covers a prepaid shipping label.

There are no fees for buying a card.

All cards must have a minimum value of $10.

When you sell a card, you get paid either via direct deposit, PayPal, or a physical check.

Amount offered for $50 Foot Locker card: No offer

Amount to buy $50 Best Buy Card: $49.75

There are others online, but these three appear to be the easiest to use, offer the most cards to both buy and sell, and are the best value for sellers.

Keep in mind, you can use the discounted gift cards in collaboration with the cash back sites mentioned in the previous chapter.

Let's say you're going to spend $100 at Gap.

eBates offers 2% cash back. Cardpool offers $100 gift cards for $85.

You buy the gift card from Cardpool for $85. Go to www.ebates .com, find the link to Gap.com, and click through. You do your shopping and spend $100, paying with the $100 gift card.

You'll receive $2 cash back from eBates, and you only paid $85 for the $100 gift card; so even though you "spent" $100 at Gap.com, it really only cost you $83.

Just remember, these discounted gift cards are just like cash when you go in the store or online. They retain their full value. You simply paid less for them. It's a great way to save money.

And if you have old gift cards collecting dust in a drawer, you can now turn them into cash.

Deal Sites

There's nothing better than saving money at stores and restaurants that you were going to visit anyway.

Sites like Groupon.com, Livingsocial.com (now owned by Groupon), and Restaurant.com offer steep discounts on restaurants. Groupon and LivingSocial also have great deals on retail, services, and travel.

All three sites require you to buy the deal in advance. Then, you can use it whenever you choose. You typically pay an amount of money up front and then redeem the deal for a higher amount later.

Here are a few examples:

On Groupon.com, I can currently buy a Groupon (the deals are called Groupons) for a car wash. It will cost me $12.99. The car wash usually costs $19.99.

I can also order $130 shoes for $29.99, or $20 worth of food at a Philly cheesesteak stand near my office for $11.

You can tailor the deals that you see for your location, whether it's home or if you're traveling.

Once you buy the Groupon, it is in your account and you can use it whenever you wish.

If there is an expiration date on the deal, you must use it by that date. Otherwise, you'll simply get the amount that you paid for it, rather than the higher value.

For example, if I bought the $20 Groupon for the cheesesteak place for $11 and use it after the expiration date, I won't get $20 worth of food, but will still be able to get the $11 worth that I paid. Your Groupon does not expire worthless.

Occasionally, you'll buy a Groupon and something will go wrong. The retailer won't honor it (that's never happened to me), the store or restaurant goes out of business (that has happened to me), or the product that you ordered was wrong (that also has happened).

I've been using Groupon for years. In every case, where either I couldn't use the Groupon or the product was not satisfactory and returnable, I received a prompt refund after I notified Groupon.

You can either have deals pushed to you via email or you can visit their site. You must have an account with Groupon to participate in a deal. It doesn't cost anything to join. You only pay when you want to buy a specific Groupon.

Most of the deals have user reviews, so if you're not sure whether to buy those shoes or go to that restaurant, you can read what other users' experiences have been like.

LivingSocial is quite similar. For example, I'm writing this in a hotel room in Las Vegas. (It's okay; I've been here for a few days. I'm over it.)

When I jump on LivingSocial.com, I see offers to pay $25 for the Eiffel Tower Experience instead of the usual $34 and pay $44 to use at a nearby spa for a treatment that normally costs $79.

Restaurant.com, as you probably guessed, offers deals on restaurants. They do have a few other discounted items, but they're likely online retailers you've never heard of. I haven't.

But the deals you get on Restaurant.com for restaurants are terrific. You can routinely buy a $25 gift certificate for $5. Occasionally, they have sales where you can get it as low as $2 for a $25 certificate.

You usually have to spend more than the certificate to be able to redeem it. For example, to use your $25 gift certificate, your bill, not including tax and tip, may have to be a minimum of $50.

So if you ate $50 worth of food and have a $25 Restaurant.com certificate that you paid $5 for, your $50 meal really cost $30.

Occasionally, the certificates cannot be used on weekends or at other times. The details are clear when you order the certificate.

Now, don't expect that the best restaurants in town will be on there or the one that's always packed. They don't need to sell discounted gift certificates. But you're likely to find some places that you know or have always wanted to try.

As I go through my local deals, there's a Mediterranean restaurant near my office that I've been to a few times that is offering $25 certificates for $10. An Indian restaurant near me is offering $15 certificates for $6 and there's even a $5 Subway certificate available for $2. However, you must spend $15 to use it.

If you want deals on merchandise, there are many coupon/deal sites, but the best one I've found is Retail Me Not (www.retailmenot.com).

When you visit Retail Me Not, you simply click on the deal that you want and it either takes you right to the retailer's site or provides you with a code to use when you check out.

Often, there are various deals from a single retailer. I'm currently looking at deals from clothing store, Forever 21. I see offers of 20% off select brands, 30% off select sport items, and 2 Girls Denim for $12.

Other deals on the site include 15% off Pier One Imports, 25% off your order on Shutterfly and 20% off at Kohl's.

Some of the deals are cash back that are paid to you via PayPal 15 to 30 days after your purchase. You must be registered with Retail Me Not and PayPal to use this feature.

As I write this, Retail Me Not is offering 20% cash back on online purchases at Macy's. So if you spend $100 at Macys.com, you'll receive $20 cash in your PayPal account.

There's a lot to explore at Retail Me Not for both online and in-store savings. If you're planning on a big day of shopping, you can save a decent amount of money.

I'm not a coupon clipper, but if I can save $20 just from a few mouse clicks, you can be sure I'll be clicking.

Travel Sites

Here's a quick word about travel sites like Expedia, Travelocity, and Hotels.com.

Personally, I've never found any great bargains on those sites that I couldn't find by going direct to the airline or hotel. This does not include package deals. You may find those cheaper on the travel sites.

But for individual flights, cars, and hotels, it will be tough to beat the airline or hotel itself.

The advantage of using Expedia and the like is that you can see many choices for flights, cars, hotels, and so on at once. And they have their own reward programs. Often, you still get credit for frequent flyer miles or hotel points and receive reward points from the site. However, this is not always the case. I've checked into many hotels booked on Expedia only to find out I would not receive my hotel reward points.

Additionally, if you book a hotel room on Expedia or one of the other aggregator sites, you are lowest priority if there is a problem.

If the hotel is overbooked, are they going to "walk" (the hotel term for moving a guest to another hotel) the guest who booked on Expedia or the one who booked directly with the hotel?

You guessed it – the Expedia customer. That's because he or she is the least profitable customer. The hotel has to pay a cut of your rate to Expedia. Plus, it knows that you're likely not a loyal customer and will use the hotel with the lowest rate you can find, regardless of the company.

I haven't seen any evidence that an airline customer is more likely to get bumped if they book on Expedia or similar sites. But again, if you're a loyal customer or frequent flyer of a particular airline, they're more likely to go out of their way to keep you happy rather than someone who booked on a travel site.

If you're a frequent traveler, you're better off sticking to one or two airlines and hotel chains and building up points and status. If you don't travel often and are simply looking for the best deal, the travel sites can point you in the right direction, but I still recommend booking directly through the airline or hotel. Particularly with the hotel, you may get a better deal if you call the property directly.

Lots of Music for Little Money

When I was a teenager, that Columbia House record deal was popular.

You'd get 12 records or tapes for a penny. And all you had to do was agree to buy one more album in the next three years.

Of course, you had to tell them not to send you a new album every month or else you'd get billed for it. But if you were conscientious like I was, you got a ton of music for not very much money.

I built my record and tape collection on Columbia House. Those vinyl records and cassettes are still in a box in my closet. I started converting them to digital via a record and cassette player that converts your music to mp3s.

You can find record or tape converters for less than $100. That way you'll have all of your favorite music on your phone or other device.

Sometimes I can even identify the song by the crackle and pop of the record before the first chord hits.

But it's a laborious process. It would take me months and probably years to convert all of my music.

Apple Music

Now, I use Apple's Music Family Membership. For $14.99 a month, my entire family has access to all of the music on Apple Music. The individual plan is $9.99 per month, or you can prepay for a year for $99. Students pay just $4.99 per month. In addition to listening to streaming music, you can download songs or albums to your phone or computer so you can listen even if you're not connected to Wi-Fi.

Apple doesn't have every song in its library, but there are 40 million of them. There haven't been too many songs that I couldn't find. Of course, you won't have the crackle and pop from when your little sister used her crayon on your Foreigner album, but it gives you a lot of music for only $14.99 per month.

The downside is that you don't own the music. So if Bruce Springsteen (or whoever owns his rights) suddenly has a disagreement with Apple and pulls his catalog, your 20 songs The Boss will disappear from your phone.

Also, if you cancel your subscription, all of your music that you downloaded through Apple Music is gone. So if you download a lot of music like I do, you're at Apple's mercy.

You also may not be able to use some of your Apple music to create a video or presentation. There are many songs for which you'll have to pay separately for a nonprotected version. They're usually only $0.99 to $1.99.

Spotify

I'm quite happy with Apple Music. But a lot of music fans who I know and respect try to convince me to switch to Spotify.

Spotify has the same price structure and roughly the same tens of millions of songs as Apple. That said, several extremely popular artists like Taylor Swift and Adele have pulled their music from Spotify (Swift allowed her music back on to Spotify in 2017) to have more control over how their music is sold and distributed.

Most artists eventually relent and return to Spotify.

Apple occasionally gets exclusives of big album releases. Those songs eventually make it to Spotify but it can take a few weeks.

One of the advantages of Spotify is that it's easier to share songs with other users than it is with Apple Music.

Both services offer playlists that are popular with music fans because they can introduce the listener to new music that they may not have heard elsewhere.

They also include personalized playlists created just for you. Most musicphiles say Spotify's playlists are better. Critics also tend to like Spotify's interface and the sound quality better than Apple Music's.

The downside of Spotify is that if you have a problem with your account, it's nearly impossible to speak to a human being. It's much easier to get a representative from Apple on the phone.

Both services can be used on iOS or Android devices.

With Spotify and Apple, you're essentially renting your music. If you cancel, you lose any of the music you've downloaded. So if there is a song you can't live without, you should buy it or, if you have it in another format, convert it to an mp3 and it's yours forever.

Amazon Music Unlimited

Amazon Prime also has a music service, but with only two million songs it has just a fraction of the content of Spotify and Apple Music.

However, Amazon offers Amazon Music Unlimited, which has tens of millions of songs. You can stream or download the songs to your device. It works well with Amazon's Alexa device.

You can ask Alexa to play a specific song or say, "Alexa, play me a sappy love song," and the next thing you know you're crying your eyes out as you sing along with Air Supply.

Amazon Music Unlimited's price is the same as Spotify and Apple Music. If you're a Prime member, it's about $2 a month less.

The service is newer than Spotify and Apple Music. Besides its easy connectivity with Alexa, there doesn't seem to be a lot of buzz about it, especially in comparison to the others.

Unless you love the idea of asking Alexa to be your personal DJ, I recommend Spotify or Apple Music. If you use an iPhone or Mac, Siri can be your DJ just as easily.

Though these services aren't perfect, the 14-year-old in me who was a member of the Columbia House Record Club loves the fact that for $99 a year, I can access all the music I want.

Amazon Prime

Unless you've been living in a cave since the 1990s, you're familiar with Amazon.com.

There's a decent chance you bought this book on Amazon. And probably a lot of other stuff over the years.

Amazon sells everything.

Need a copy of a new best seller? Check.

Out of Vidalia onion salad dressing? Amazon's got it.

Need your gutters cleaned? Amazon can help you book someone to do that too.

You name it, Amazon carries it. And usually at excellent prices.

Not only that, its customer service is pretty solid. Returns are easy. So is using gift cards.

This may sound like a commercial for Amazon.com. I don't own the stock – not until they start paying a strong dividend. And I assure you I don't receive any compensation from the company. In fact, just the opposite. Much of my compensation goes right to Amazon as my family orders something from Amazon every day.

Every. Single. Day.

I'm not kidding. If the UPS driver doesn't come by one day, I get worried something happened to him.

While I prefer to shop locally, especially at family-owned stores, with two kids and a demanding job, it's not always possible. Sometimes (often) we just need the convenience of ordering it online.

So if you order stuff online somewhat regularly, it is worth your while to look at upgrading your Amazon account to Amazon Prime.

Let's take a closer look at the service so you can decide if it's right for you.

First of all, the cost of Amazon Prime is $99 per year.

What do you get for that $99?

1) Free Shipping

Without Prime, you usually have to spend $49 to get free shipping (or $25 on books). Otherwise, you'll have to pay for getting the package delivered to you. If you order something at least once a month for less than $49, you could easily spend $50 a year on shipping.

Most of what you buy from Amazon will be eligible for free two-day shipping with a Prime membership. However, occasionally you may order from an independent vendor doing business through Amazon. In that case, your purchase may not receive free shipping. If that happens, it will clearly be marked not eligible for Amazon Prime, and you'll see the shipping charge before you submit the order.

2) Streaming Content

With Amazon Prime you have unlimited access to more than one million songs and thousands of playlists/stations that you can play for free.

Additionally, Amazon is challenging Netflix and the cable networks in creating its own television shows, some of which are excellent.

My son and I were glued to *The Man in the High Castle* for two seasons. Amazon gets some big names involved in their shows like Woody Allen, John Goodman, and Jeffrey Tambor.

3) Prime Photos

This may be the most important perk. With Amazon Prime, you get unlimited storage of your digital photos. You also receive 5GB of storage for video and other documents.

To me, this is almost worth the cost alone. I store my photos on a back-up drive at home, but if something happened to my computer and the drive, like a house fire, I'd lose all my photos.

With Amazon Prime Photos, I can upload all my pictures so that if anything ever happened to my equipment, they are safe in an offsite location.

Combine this service with the free shipping and I'm on board.

But as they say on TV, "Wait, there's more . . . "

4) Kindle Owners Lending Library

If you read on a Kindle, as an Amazon Prime member you can borrow one e-book per month for free. There is no due date to return it, though you can't borrow another until you do.

There are also other things you can borrow from Amazon Prime Reading, like magazines such as *Sports Illustrated, Cosmopolitan*, and *Car & Driver.*

5) Prime Now

If you're in one of 32 cities (adding more all the time) across the U.S., including Dallas, Washington, D.C., and San Francisco, you can get groceries (and 25,000 other items like electronics) delivered to your door for free in two hours.

The minimum order is $35.

Additionally, you can get free delivery from restaurants with a minimum $20 order.

Having a dinner party and burned the roast? (Does anyone make roasts at dinner parties anymore?) No problem. Log on to Amazon Prime Now and order dinner from that Italian place you love a few miles away.

At the same time, ask Amazon to bring over a bottle of Pinot Noir, some brownies for dessert, and the air conditioner filters you forgot to buy earlier today.

What's also nice about this service is if you have a friend who is sick, recovering from surgery, or can't get out of the house for any other reason, it's easy to send over a meal from their favorite restaurant or some groceries. That way, if you can't get there right away or even if you live out of town, you can be good friend and help them out.

There are some other benefits that are mostly deal related. You'll get first crack at certain money-saving offers. Those are nice but I find I don't use them.

The benefits I've highlighted are, in my opinion, worth the $99.

In fact, as I'm writing this, I'm realizing I'm not taking enough advantage of my Prime membership. I have to start using the streaming music service and lending library more.

You can try Amazon Prime for free for 30 days to see if you like it. If you don't, no sweat. Just let them know within 30 days, and you won't be charged. Keep in mind, at that point you won't have unlimited photo storage anymore, so make sure your photos are backed up somewhere before you cancel.

To sign up or explore all of the benefits plus the terms and conditions, visit www.amazon.com and click on Amazon Prime for more information.

If you're anything like me, you'll save more than $99 per year and get fun and convenient services as well.

Take Great Classes for Free (or Close to Free)

This section isn't about how to send a kid to college for free. I'm still trying to figure that out since neither of my kids can hit a three-point shot.

But 18-year-olds aren't the only ones that want to learn things.

Taking courses is a favorite pastime for many retirees. Not only does it keep their minds active, which has been shown to hold off the effects of age-related dementia, but retirees finally have the time to pursue those interests that they couldn't while they were focused on their careers and families.

I would love to learn Italian cooking. But with two kids, a job, and the deadline for this book rapidly approaching, that's not happening any time soon.

In fact, for some, one of the appealing things about retirement is finally having the time to learn new skills and follow those dreams that have been stuffed away for so long.

If you want to learn Italian cooking, you could go to Tuscany and take private lessons. But that's a little pricey.

Instead, you might be able to take a course for free or at an extremely affordable price.

Community College

Community college isn't just for kids starting their college careers. You don't need to be going for a degree to take a class at a community college. If there is something that the college offers that interests you, take a class. Don't worry about the grade, the assignments, and so on. You're an adult. You're taking the class because you're interested, not because you need the grade or credit.

Depending on the school and the course, classes usually run about $75 to $150. While many of the classes are designed to prepare students for careers, there are plenty of art, history, cooking, science, and other classes sure to meet some of your interests.

When I was first starting out and had little money, I wanted to learn how to play golf. But golf lessons are expensive.

Fortunately, City College of San Francisco had a beginning golf class. My wife and I both enrolled. I think we paid about $40 each.

We showed up when we wanted to and learned the basics. I wasn't exactly ready to go pro when it was over but at least knew how to grip and swing a club.

Was it awkward being with mostly 19-year-old kids who were earning an easy physical education credit? Maybe a little, though there were a few others like us in the class. But any slight awkwardness was made up for the fact that we were getting golf lessons for pennies on the dollar.

Let's take a look at some courses available at a few different community colleges around the U.S.

At Mott Community College in Flint, Michigan, you can learn Arabic or Chinese and get an introduction to computer programming.

At Clackamas Community College in Oregon City, Oregon, students can take photography, line dancing, and organic gardening.

And at Whatcom Community College in Bellingham, Washington, courses include Computer Security and Virus Protection for the Home User, creative writing, and first aid for pets.

Chances are, you'll be able to find something you're interested in at a community college. Many of them offer adult education classes and if not, you can usually audit a class. That way you're not paying for or enrolled in a degree program.

By the way, if you want to go back to school to earn a degree, the Plus 50 Program is a terrific initiative to help train students age 50 and older for new careers – particularly the kind that give back to the community such as education, nursing assistants, and substance abuse counselors.

Plus 50 is offered at community colleges and is designed to help students find jobs quickly. So if you're not ready to take golf or Italian cooking classes, but want to be out there helping your community and earning income at the same time, Plus 50 might help.

Call your local community college or visit its website to see if it has a Plus 50 program.

Lastly, it's kind of fun being on a college campus. There's something about being around all of that youth and optimism that can't help but rub off on you.

If you're unable to find what you're looking for at a community college but have a state college or even private university nearby, see what options they have for seniors or adult education. You'll be surprised at how affordable it may be to take classes at even prestigious institutions of higher learning.

Community-Based Adult Education Programs

Many towns and counties offer classes for adults that are unaffiliated with a college. Classes are often taught at high schools or other public schools during the evening and are quite inexpensive.

For example, Palm Beach County, Florida, offers a variety of classes such as ceramics, Adobe Photoshop, and gourmet cooking. These classes meet once a week for six to eight weeks and cost about $75.

And like my golf experience, there's no pressure. You're not trying to graduate at the top of your class. If you can't make it one week, no problem. Plus, you'll meet other people who are interested in the same things you are, which is always a bonus.

If you're not sure where to look, do a Google search for adult education in your area.

iTunes U

The list of things that I want to learn is long.

A foreign language, how to play the harmonica, and how to be a better poker player are just a few.

So imagine my delight when I discovered online courses, particularly ones that are free and are at my own pace.

The first thing I did was download a course on Game Theory from Yale University. Here I was, watching this class for free that the kids in the classroom had paid thousands for. Better yet, I could watch it whenever I wanted or scroll back if I missed something that the professor said. I didn't have homework, worry about grades, or get distracted by a pretty brunette in the third row. Yet, I was still taking a Yale University class.

One of the best sources for free quality online classes is the Open University on iTunes U.

In my opinion, iTunes U is the best-kept secret on the internet. Everyone knows about Apple's phones, computers, iPads, and probably iTunes, which offer music and video. But within iTunes, lies this gem – iTunes U.

If you visit www.open.edu/itunes you will find hundreds of courses from hundreds of universities around the world in an expansive list of subjects – all for free if you have an iTunes account (which is also free).

The list of courses is fascinating. In the languages section, they have Spanish, French, and German, but also have "The Language of Comedy" – 12 three- or four-minute lessons on how jokes are crafted. I just downloaded that one, so the rest of this book should be much funnier.

There's an eight-class course on Personal Finance from Missouri State University. The classes range from 5 to 45 minutes.

And if you only want to take classes from Yale, there are more than 150 to choose from including courses on the Middle Ages, organic chemistry, and a 22-part seminar on autism.

Apple doesn't really promote iTunes U as a benefit of having an iTunes account, probably because almost all of the content is free. But it's hard to find a better benefit. All of this knowledge from universities from around the planet at your fingertips – for free.

This really is an amazing time to be alive.

Sorry, I got caught up in the moment. And while writing this chapter, I've found so many classes I want to download and take at my leisure.

To access iTunes U, you need iTunes. On your phone or iPad, click on the blue icon with the "A" on it. That's the App Store. Search for iTunes U and download the app. On your Mac computer, the courses are listed in the podcasts section of iTunes.

If you have an Android or PC, you'll have to download the iTunes app, which is free.

Other Online Classes

It's hard to imagine you won't be able to find what you're looking for at iTunes U. But if that should occur, there are other places to take online classes. Most universities and colleges offer them, though you will likely have to pay a fee.

There are plenty of free online classes available as well.

Search free online classes for an idea of what's out there.

When I googled "Free Online Classes," the first thing that came up was a list of courses from Harvard including a class about science in cooking taught by chefs, a class on Shakespeare, and a Chinese history course.

There are many free resources out there that you'll discover with a simple Google search. And if you know specifically what you want to learn, type that into your Google search bar.

When I type in "free online Italian cooking class," again, there are many to choose from including this one from Massachusetts Institute of Technology, "Speak Italian With Your Mouth Full," where students learn to speak basic Italian while learning to cook an Italian dish.

The only downside to online courses, particularly the free ones that you download, is that there is no social aspect to it. You're not interacting with classmates, and you typically can't contact the professor for help. And some classes like "Speak Italian With Your Mouth Full" may be fun to take with another person or a group.

But if you have a thirst for knowledge, community colleges, adult education courses, and free online classes should be able to keep you inundated with fascinating lectures, presentations, and maybe even some homework.

And the best part is, you don't have to do your homework if you don't want. No one is going to send a note home saying you're falling behind on your assignments.

So stay up late, go to that party, and come to class whenever you please.

If only junior year had been like that.

Actions to Take

- Shop online using reward sites, or you're leaving cash on the table.
- Never pay full price for a gift card again.
- Amazon is taking over the world. For good reason, Amazon Prime is a great deal.
- Take classes, especially Italian cooking – and then invite me over for dinner. I'll bring the Chianti.

PART

IV

Ideas I Don't Like

"I don't like people who hide things."

– Grace Jones

This last section of *You Don't Have to Drive an Uber in Retirement* is about common, even popular strategies that many retirees use to generate income...

But most of them are rip offs.

These methods can generate income, but usually at a very high price. You can do much better investing your money in other ways. You'll have a larger nest egg, generate more income, and leave more to your family if you stay away from the methods in this section.

No one cares more about your money than you. Do you know who doesn't really care about your money? Most sales people that sell financial products. They care about *their* money, which they make selling you over-priced, often ineffective products and services.

Remember that nothing in life is guaranteed. If you're getting a guarantee on a financial product, it's because you're paying through the nose for it.

Some people might be OK with that. They need the peace of mind that comes with a guarantee no matter how expensive it is.

But I believe most people can do better on their own or with a professional who will act as a fiduciary.

If a financial professional is a fiduciary, it means they are required by law to act in the client's best interest.

Surprisingly, many financial professionals are not fiduciaries and don't have to act in the client's best interest. They may sell you expensive insurance plans or other products even if it's not the best thing for you. It may be the best thing for *them* as they get a large commission.

Certified Financial Planners (CFPs) are fiduciaries. Your run-of-the-mill stockbroker and insurance salesperson is not.

There are plenty of honest stockbrokers and insurance salespeople who do the right thing by their clients. But there are plenty who don't. So if you're working with someone who is not a fiduciary, you better be sure they're looking out for your interests and not trying to make a down payment on a boat.

I'm going to get a lot of pushback for criticizing the strategies in the next three chapters. Some of these are programs you may already be participating in.

Just remember, I'm not selling anything here. You've already bought the book. My only motivation is to keep you from spending your hard-earned money on financial products that are likely not in your best interest.

16

The Worst Investment You Can Make

"The point is, how do you know the Guarantee Fairy isn't a crazy glue sniffer?"

– Chris Farley

I'm going to lose some friends on this one because I know people who sell annuities.

But if you learn only one thing from this book – it should be this: Don't buy annuities.

Granted, annuities aren't wrong for everyone – just most everyone.

If you're unfamiliar with annuities – you give an insurance company your money, then they promise to pay you an income stream, usually for the rest of your life. In some annuities, if you die before you've received all of your money back, too bad for you.

I'll re-use the Willy Wonka quote from the Introduction: "You get nothing! You lose! Good day, sir!"

Seriously, that's how it works.

Let's say you're a 60-year-old who wants to start receiving an income at 70 for the rest of your life. You give the insurance company a chunk of money but at age 69, you pass away. Your money is gone. Your family doesn't get a dime.

Now, there are plenty of annuities where that's not the case. Family members can receive cash back or even continued monthly income – but you pay for that.

Essentially, you're betting the insurance company that you're going to live longer than they think you will. They take your money, invest it, and give it back to you in dribs and drabs (with steep penalties if you want to withdraw more than the contract states).

They have figured out how long you're going to live. It doesn't matter if you practice yoga every day and eat nothing but yogurt and salad. Their Ivy League PhDs have a pretty good idea on how to bet against your life and make money for them.

Annuities are such terrible investments that the minute the government passed a law specifying that financial professionals had to act in their clients' best interest, annuity sales fell off a cliff.

In 2016, new rules were passed by the Department of Labor that stated that brokers must act as fiduciaries. As I mentioned in the introduction to Part IV, that means they have to put their clients' best interest ahead of their own.

Believe it or not, prior to the rule being passed, stock and insurance brokers could sell you anything they wanted whether it was right for you or not. So, typically, they sold whatever had the highest commissions.

Annuities pay extremely high commissions – often 7% or higher of the total amount. So if a client was sold a $200,000 annuity, the salesperson might take home $14,000, up front.

There's not a lot of incentive for him to put you in a low-cost index fund if he can make $14,000 from one sale.

This new law was scheduled to go fully into effect in 2018. However, the Trump administration delayed its implementation until July, 2019 and is reviewing the regulations with the likely intent of getting rid of the law entirely. This will leave unsuspecting consumers to be preyed upon by financial "professionals" who are only concerned with meeting their own mortgage payment, not their clients'.

As soon as the fiduciary rule was passed, sales of annuities fell 8% in 2016[1] and slid 18% in the first quarter of 2017.[2]

Sales of variable annuities, which are the worst of the worst, crashed 22% in 2016.

---

[1] http://www.irionline.org/research/research-detail-view/iri-issues-fourth-quarter-2016-annuity-sales-report.

[2] https://www.myirionline.org/newsroom/newsroom-detail-view/iri-issues-first-quarter-2017-annuity-sales-report.

If these were such wonderful products, as defenders of annuities maintain, why did so many people stop selling them – even before the law went into effect?

So Why Do People Like Them?

I've met many annuity investors who are happy. They're aware of the costs associated with their annuity, but appreciate the peace of mind that comes with knowing their principal is protected (in many cases).

Fixed annuities prevent any losses. You are typically guaranteed that the value of your principal will not go down no matter what the stock or bond markets do. (That guarantee is only as good as the insurance company that wrote the contract, but most insurance companies are in solid shape.)

Fixed index annuities allow the investor to take part in some upside, though it is usually very limited – about 4% per year in this low interest rate environment. So the investor is trading upside potential for downside protection.

If the market soars 20%, the investor will only make 4%. But if the market falls 20%, the investor won't lose any money.

Other annuities offer more upside potential but with more downside risk. You can probably find an annuity with any kind of terms you want. If you're willing to risk 5% of your capital in exchange for greater upside potential, someone will write that contract. Ten percent risk with even more participation in the upside? Shouldn't be a problem.

Obviously, if you have no downside protection and the market falls, your nest egg will generate less income, which is the whole point of an annuity. Annuities allow investors to lock in an income stream and ensure their capital is protected.

They pay through the nose for that peace of mind, but for some people it's worth it.

Because annuity salesmen have a reputation that's down there with used car salesmen and politicians, the industry is trying to address it by offering annual fees instead of a commission.

But there's a big problem with that plan.

Let's assume the annual fee is 1%, similar to what most brokers or planners will charge to manage your money.

If you are working with a broker or planner and have a $200,000 account, the money manager will typically keep some of your capital in cash so that they can pay themselves the 1% or $2,000 per year. If they don't, they'll sell some of your liquid investments in order to raise the cash to pay themselves.

An annuity has very strict terms on how much money is to be paid out/withdrawn each year. If somehow you were able to get the money out of the annuity to pay the fee, it would lower the income you'll receive because the guaranteed income stream is based on how much capital is in the account.

So if you start taking out $2,000 per year, that means there is less money in the annuity to grow or accrue interest on.

Additionally, it may be even more expensive to pay an annual fee, even one as low as 1%.

If you take out a $200,000 annuity and pay that 7% commission (by the way, they'll never tell you they're receiving such a large commission), you'll pay $14,000.

Instead, if you pay a 1% annual fee, after ten years, you'll have paid $20,000.

So annual fees are hardly the answer.

The answer is – don't buy these B.S. products.

Instead, take the money and invest it in Perpetual Dividend Raisers – companies that raise their dividend every year.

"But I don't want to risk any money," you say. "After all, that's one of the most attractive features of annuities."

Annuities are typically long-term contracts. People buy them in their 60s, 70s and even 80s, expecting to collect income for years in the future.

Consider that over 10-year periods, the stock market has only been down seven times in the past 80 years. And those seven times all were tied to either the Great Depression or Great Recession.

In other words, you had to sell in the depths of historic financial collapses to not make money in the stock market over 10 years.

If you invested in 2000, near the top of the dot-com bubble, and sold in 2009, near the bottom of the Great Recession, you were down 9%. Not good, but not horrendous considering you'd have endured two epic stock market meltdowns.

Or consider this scenario: If you have the worst timing and put your nest egg into the S&P 500 at the absolute top in 2007, right before the financial collapse, a little less than 10 years later, you'd be up 91% including dividends.

Just stop and think about that for a second the next time market naysayers or those who try to scare you out of stocks talk about the "Wall Street casino."

Investing at the all-time high and watching the market crater would have been no fun. But if you'd held on, you'd have nearly doubled your money over ten years.

So you'd need incredibly bad timing getting into the market and even worse timing getting out to not make money over 10 years.

Annuity contracts typically last for many years. If you buy an annuity in your 60s or 70s, chances are you're trying to secure your income until at least 90 years old and maybe longer.

So you might be looking at locking your money up for 20 years in the annuity.

The stock market has never been down over any 20-year period.

That doesn't mean it can't happen. The stock market is not guaranteed. But we have more than a century of history to look back on and we know that – over the long term – markets go higher.

On June 26, 2017, Barron's published a list of The 50 Best Annuities.[3] Let's take a look at the top one in each category and compare it to a portfolio of Perpetual Dividend Raisers that uses my 10-11-12 System.

My 10-11-12 System was featured in my first book, *Get Rich with Dividends*. It is designed to generate 11% yields in 10 years or, if dividends are reinvested, 12% average annual total returns over 10 years.

Immediate Income

Barron's top immediate income, life-only annuity was offered by Minnesota Life. An immediate income, life-only annuity is where an investor starts collecting income immediately and if they die, the insurance company keeps the money.

On a $200,000 investment, a 70-year-old male would collect $15,564 per year over 20 years, a total of $311,280 (assuming he lived that long).

Because my system needs time to let compounding work its magic, the investor would not collect as much income immediately

---

[3] *Barron's*, June 26, 2017, pp 19–24.

as he would with an annuity. It wouldn't be until year six that he'd earn the full $15,564 per year.

However, by year 14 he'd receive $32,260, more than double the amount paid by the annuity.

So if the investor needed $15,000 per year in income starting immediately, my system would not be the way to go unless he could fund the difference from another source until the payments catch up.

But it might be worth trying because if the portfolio simply achieved the historical market average growth rate, after 10 years, it would be worth $417,994. The investor could start to take a lot more money out then – and with no penalties or restrictions. It's his money. He can do whatever he wants with it.

After 20 years, the portfolio would be worth $873,596.

That's including normal bull, bear, and flat markets over 20 years.

	Immediate income annuity	10-11-12 System
Annual income in year 1	$15,564	$9,400
Annual income in year 20	$15,564	$56,995
Average annual income	$15,564	$26,766
Total income received after 20 years	$311,280	$535,377
Portfolio value after 20 years	$0	$873,596

The big benefit is that when the investor passes away, his family receives all of the money. Not only do they get the principal back, but the entire portfolio, which could be worth hundreds of thousands of dollars.

Also, imagine the healthy 70-year-old puts the $200,000 into an annuity, collects his $15,000 a year as long as he lives, and at 90 needs to move into a nursing home. The $15,000 per year will help, but not much.

The 10-11-12 System portfolio is now worth more than $800,000, spinning off nearly $57,000 per year, thanks to the power of compounding. That $57,000 will help defray the cost. Plus, the family has more than $873,000 that can be used as well (though any liquidation of the portfolio will lower the annual income).

So the family has a lot more options.

Barron's listed two other categories of immediate income annuities: "10 Year Certain" annuities, where the heirs continue to get paid for 10 years if the investor dies within the first 10 years; and a "cash installment refund" annuity, where the family receives the remaining principal paid out monthly.

In both of those cases, the investor receives less monthly income and total income paid out over 20 years – if he makes it that long.

Deferred Income

A deferred income annuity is where you put money away for a specific number of years, let it build up interest, and then begin receiving income from the now larger investment capital.

Barron's top-ranked deferred income annuity, sometimes known as a personal pension, is from Lincoln National Life.

The example assumes a 60-year-old male invests $200,000 and begins withdrawing income at age 70. He receives income until death. If there is any remaining principal left after death, it will go to his heirs.

At age 70, the investor begins receiving a guaranteed $21,015. By age 90, he has cashed checks totaling $420,300. At his death at the age of 90, his family receives nothing.

Instead, if the he invests in the 10-11-12 System but reinvests the dividends over 10 years (since he doesn't need the income until he's 70 and can let the portfolio's growth accelerate due to compounding), his $200,000 would be worth $692,914.

At this point, he stops reinvesting the dividend and begins to withdraw the dividend income that it spins off. (Note, he is not touching the principal, just the dividends.)

He's already ahead of the game in year one, as he will receive $32,566. That's around $11,000 more than the annuity.

Because the dividends continue to be raised every year, the investor is getting paid a whopping $197,463 at the age of 90.

The average payment was $92,735 and he collected $1,854,714 in 20 years. That's nearly a million and a half dollars more than the annuity.

And at his death at age 90 1/2, his family inherits $3,026,634, versus bupkus for the annuity investor's family.

	Deferred income annuity	10-11-12 System
Annual income in year 1	$21,015	$32,566
Annual income in year 20	$21,015	$197,463
Average annual income	$21,015	$92,735
Total income received after 20 years	$420,300	$1,854,714
Portfolio value after 20 years	$0	$3,026,634

That is a hell of a difference.

Now of course, the 10-11-12 System isn't guaranteed the way an annuity is. The results could be less or they could be more. Let's say the numbers are only half as good as what I've outlined here. You still come out way ahead of an annuity.

And remember, the market has never gone down over 20 years. And if it does, so what? You're not using that money to pay the bills. You're living off of the dividends. Just because a stock goes down doesn't mean its dividend decreases.

There are several hundred companies that raised their dividends, even during the market meltdown in 2008–2009, while their stock prices were falling. And there are many others that maintained their dividend.

Keep in mind, this comparison was done with the very best annuities that Barron's could find. Imagine the difference between the average annuity and investing in Perpetual Dividend Raisers.

Another Way They Screw You

Let's say you take out an annuity and your circumstances change. You need the money urgently. If you're still within the surrender period, it's going to cost you. Big.

A typical surrender period is seven years, and the surrender charge starts at 7% and falls by 1% per year.

So if after two years, you need your money back, it's going to cost you $10,000 ($200,000 × 5% = $10,000) . . . to get your own money back.

If you have the money in the stock market, it will cost you about $9.95 (or whatever your discount broker charges) to sell stock.

It's important to understand that in two years, stock prices could be anywhere. If we're in the middle of a correction or bear market in year two when you need the cash, your portfolio might be worth less than the $200,000 you originally put in.

So you shouldn't invest in the market expecting to take money out within a few years. This is a long-term strategy, especially compared to an annuity.

Of course, the market could be higher, and you can take out the money you need and let the rest build and generate income.

But you get the point that no one is going to penalize you for taking out your own money.

Actions to Take

- Don't buy annuities unless you don't mind paying ridiculously high prices for underperformance and guarantees.
- If you are considering an annuity, do a comparison as to how much income and total return you'd likely earn in the stock market over the same period of time.
- Prepare your family that they may not see a penny of that annuity money after you're gone.
- Remember, if annuities are so wonderful, why did annuity salespeople scurry like cockroaches when you turn the light on – even before the fiduciary law went into effect?

CHAPTER 17

Lose Your Life Insurance

"Fun is like life insurance; the older you get, the more it costs."

– Kin Hubbard

This chapter may lose me a few more friends – particularly those who sell life insurance for a living.

You see, over the past ten years, I've written quite a bit about why life insurance as an investment is a scam.

Life insurance should be used to insure your future earnings in the event of your untimely death. Anything other than that and you are flushing money down the toilet.

When my wife got pregnant with our first child, I immediately went shopping for term life insurance. I wanted to make sure Junior could go to college if something happened to either of us. Because my wife and I were young and healthy, our premiums were cheap. Combined, we pay about $1,000 per year for $1 million policies.

That was 16 years ago. The policies expire in four years. So now I've been thinking about whether to extend them. My daughter will graduate college in nine years (assuming she's on the four-year plan, which she better be).

To get a $1 million policy today it would cost me at least $1,500 per year or $30,000 over the 20-year term. Same with my wife.

The question is, do we really need it?

If something happens to me in the next 20 years, that $1 million will sure be helpful to my family. But am I willing to wager $30,000 on it? All four of my grandparents lived to at least 85. Three of them lived into their 90s.

That's certainly no guarantee I'll live that long. But if I avoid a bad accident and don't do anything stupid (always a possibility), it's a good indicator that I should live past 70.

We took a look at our family finances and determined that should I take a dirt nap after my initial policy expires, but while my daughter is in college, she could afford to stay in school. We've been saving for her college in a 529 plan since she was born.

Additionally, my wife could turn some of our investments into income-producing assets. Lastly, she works. If she's able to continue to work, she can still put food on the table even without using our investments for income.

As for funeral expenses, I told my wife to get the cheapest pine box she can find. Heck, put me in a cardboard box from U-Haul for all I care. Who do I have to impress at that point? Do it as inexpensively as possible.

So we determined we would "self insure," which basically means not insure.

Not everyone is in the same situation. If certain needs (tuition, living expenses, etc.) cannot be met without the income from your job or business, then term life insurance is a very good idea.

But if your family can meet those expenses without a life insurance payout, you're probably better off saving the money and investing it.

If instead of paying $1,500 per year to an insurance company, I invest it in the S&P 500 and achieve its historical return, at the end of 20 years, I should have $77,642.

If I'm able to obtain the 12% average annual total return of my 10-11-12 System, I'll nearly double that figure and wind up with $135,517.

So I'd rather keep the $30,000 over 20 years and try to quadruple it.

If you are concerned about your family not being able to pay its bills in the event of your death, term life is an excellent solution. It's usually fairly inexpensive and can help your loved ones deal with your demise without the burden of worrying about how to fund future expenses.

Whole Life

So I'm good with term life insurance if you need it.

On the other hand, a whole life policy is one of the worst things you can do with your money (besides annuities). If you're considering getting a whole life policy, just take your insurance broker to the car dealer of his or her choice and put down the down payment on the car they want. At least you'll get the satisfaction of seeing them smile as they drive away in the car you just bought them.

Because when you buy a whole life policy, you're basically doing that anyway. And you're getting very little in return.

I can feel my future inbox filling up with angry emails. It always does when I write negatively about whole life insurance. But I don't care. I don't want you to waste your money on one of these junk policies.

Whole life policies are sold as an investment. It's a way to make your money grow, but it also has a life insurance component.

For the sake of brevity, in this chapter I will use whole life to represent any insurance product that has a cash value, such as universal life.

Some people think whole life policies are more attractive than term life. That's because with a term life insurance policy, if you are alive when the policy expires, the insurance company keeps all of the money.

In my case, at nearly $1,000 per year for 20 years, I'll have paid the insurer $20,000 and will have nothing to show for it – other than peace of mind over those 20 years, which is certainly worth something, maybe even $1,000 per year.

But that rubs some people the wrong way. The insurance company keeps it all, and you have nothing to show for it after diligently paying premiums for those many years.

With a whole life policy, there is a death benefit if you pass away. If you don't die, your money is there for you as it has been invested and presumably is worth more than when you invested it (assuming the markets cooperate).

My question is why not just buy a term life insurance policy and invest the rest the way you see fit – rather than in an expensive investment fund that will most likely underperform the market (as the vast majority of funds do)?

Here's how a whole life policy works:

When you buy a whole life policy (or any policy where there is cash value), part of your premium goes to pay for the insurance and the rest is invested. Policies can have fixed-rate guarantees or they can vary depending on the performance of the stock market. The variable policies typically have ceilings as to how much you can earn in a given year, but also have guarantees that you won't lose anything.

So if the market goes up 20% in a year, you may only earn 6% if that's your cap. But if the market crashes, you won't lose anything.

Now, I misspoke (miswrote?). When I said the rest of your premium is invested, that's not quite accurate. A good chunk of it goes to pay commissions to the salesperson and fees to the insurance company.

In fact, whole life insurance premiums are typically three to five times those of term life. Of course, some of that is going toward your investment, but too much of it goes to someone else.

When an insurance agent sells you a whole life policy, his commission is typically your entire first year premium. Then, he usually earns 7% of your premiums after.[1]

That's a lot of your money that is *not* going toward your cash value.

From purely an insurance perspective, the nice thing about whole life is that your premiums will never go up as long as you pay your premium every month and don't let it lapse.

That's no matter how old you are or what your health condition is.

If you're a 40-year-old who takes out a whole life policy with a $250 monthly premium and you keep the policy current, it will remain $250 per month until you withdraw funds or pass away.

On the other hand, if you take out a 20-year term policy at 40 and then decide you want to keep the insurance for another 10 years, your premium will be higher after year 20.

Of course, it will be lower than a whole life policy, but it will be higher than you had been paying for term life.

---

[1]https://www.nerdwallet.com/blog/insurance/life-insurance-agent-commissions/.

Show Me the Money

The reason a person would take out a whole life policy is for the cash value. At a certain point, the policyholder will be able to withdraw funds. Depending on how much he or she contributes and the rate of return, there could be a nice little cash stash there.

Just as I showed you in the last chapter about annuities, the best (and cheapest) way to build your nest egg over the long term is to invest in stocks that raise the dividend every year.

That's because the low commissions and fees of investing on your own will generate higher returns than an insurance product disguised as an investment. (Or is it an investment product disguised as insurance?)

No one is taking 7% of your money and putting it in their pocket when you buy a stock.

Remember, stocks go up over the long term. You need historically terrible timing to not make money in the markets over 10 years. And the markets have never lost money over 20 years.

Whole life policies are long-term investments. You don't just pay your premium for three years and then decide you don't like the market right now, so you're not going to pay this month. If that happens, your policy lapses. You lose the insurance component and depending on the policy and when you let it lapse, may have to pay exorbitant fees (as much as 10% of your cash value).

The Taxman

One of the arguments I routinely hear about whole life policies is that the cash value grows without taxation. You are only taxed if your withdrawals from the policy exceed what you put into it.

Well, that's the whole point – to take more money out than you put in. That's why you invest in anything.

With a whole life policy, you may be able to defer the taxes a bit longer than with a regular investment.

If you invested $50,000 in a whole life policy, the cash value grows to $100,000 and you withdraw $10,000 per year, you'd likely not pay any taxes until year six – when your total withdrawals have exceeded your contribution.

Instead, if you invested $50,000 in stocks, the portfolio grew to $100,000, and you sold $10,000 worth to be able to withdraw the cash, you'd likely have to pay capital gains taxes on the withdrawn funds.

Additionally, some policies pay dividends. Those dividends grow tax deferred as well – with the same rules applying: Once total withdrawals exceed contributions, the funds are taxed.

If you're investing in stocks, dividends are taxed in the year received, even if you're reinvesting them and don't receive the cash.

However, if the stock is held in an IRA or 401k, the taxes are deferred until withdrawal.

One of my issues with whole life policies is the tax advantage can quickly become a difficult situation.

If you are regularly saving and investing in stocks, an IRA, or 401k and times suddenly get tough, you can stop investing for a little while until you get on your feet.

With a whole life policy, once you stop paying your premium, your policy lapses and you could be charged fees. Then, if you want to take your money out early, you're charged more fees.

And that tax advantage can really backfire.

Let's say you have contributed $40,000 toward a policy that now has a cash value of $60,000. You lose your job or have some big unexpected costs, so you withdraw the money early.

Even if you don't have any surrender charges, you are now on the hook for taxes on the excess $20,000. It wasn't a slow methodical withdrawal like you expected when you started the policy. Life happened, you need the money, and now the IRS is going to take a chunk; and it doesn't care that you lost your job, ended up in the hospital, or unexpectedly needed a new roof.

Don't Bank on Yourself

Lastly, I have an enormous issue with the "bank on yourself" movement.

This is a strategy promoted mostly by people who sell life insurance policies.

The idea is that you can borrow against your cash value. It is often sold as a tax-free withdrawal. If you have a cash value of $100,000 and "borrowed" $10,000 of it, you're taking your money out without paying taxes.

But you will pay interest since it is technically a loan. The interest rate is typically fairly low, about what you'd get from a bank.

However, if the loan is not managed properly, it can become taxable.

The interest on the loan is often paid out of the remaining cash value. If the accrued interest is larger than the remaining cash value, the investor either needs to put more money into the policy immediately or the policy will lapse. At the point the policy lapses, the loan becomes taxable.

So now you've taken out a loan on which you owe interest *and* created a taxable event.

Whole Life – Who Is It Good For?

I bet you thought I'd say absolutely no one ... and that I'd say it again.

I will concede that a whole life policy isn't a bad idea for everyone. But like annuities, it is bad for nearly everyone.

A whole life policy needs to be held and funded for decades if it's going to work.

According to actuary James Hunt, who has analyzed thousands of policies for the Consumer Federation of America, whole life policies hardly ever offered a reasonable return unless held for at least 20 years.[2]

A study by Mass Mutual backed up Hunt's statement. These policies typically earn between 4.59% and 6.52% annually over 28 years compared to 8% to 10% in the stock market.[3]

I have run my own comparisons of whole life policies to a portfolio of Perpetual Dividend Raisers, and you always wind up with more money with the Perpetual Dividend Raisers, assuming the stocks return the historical market average. Over 20 or 30 years, that's a pretty good bet.

And the stock investor will save tens of thousands of dollars in commissions and fees. That's money that can continue to compound and turn into more money for you rather than turn into a life insurance salesman's Audi.

A whole life policy can work for two types of individuals.

The first is someone who is young and plans to hold the policy for decades – at least 20 years and preferably 30 or more. During that

---

[2]http://www.investmentu.com/article/detail/33809/when-death-is-the-best-investment#.WVLcKVI1RPM.

[3]https://www.forbes.com/sites/financialfinesse/2012/07/11/how-high-income-earners-can-protect-themselves-from-rising-taxes/#7a38d41465dd.

time, the policyholder must not miss a payment, need the money, or let the policy lapse for any reason. Otherwise, they will be on the hook for more fees and taxes.

The problem is, most people don't keep making those payments over the decades. More than 25% of all whole life policies lapse within the first three years.[4] That means those folks poured lighter fluid on their cash and lit a match.

Now, you could argue the same would have happened with a term life policy. That's true, but the difference is over those three years a customer with term life likely would be down anywhere from less than a thousand dollars to two or three thousand.

Someone who let a whole life policy lapse after three years has probably squandered at least $10,000 and probably a lot more.

As I've said, that person is better off investing in a portfolio of companies that raise their dividends every year – especially if it's in an IRA or 401k. However, with a tax-deferred retirement account, there is a limit to how much you can invest – currently that figure is $5,500 up to age 49 or $6,500 for 50 and older in an IRA.

Employees in a 401k, 403b, or the Federal government's Thrift Savings Plan can contribute $18,500 younger than age 50 and $24,500 if they're 50 and older.[5]

But if you want to save more for retirement than the government will allow in a 401k or IRA, a whole life policy will compound tax deferred. You can contribute as much as you want.

Remember, you'll still pay taxes once you withdraw more than you've contributed, but that may be a long way off.

Whole life polices are really best suited for very wealthy people who want to protect their assets from the estate tax.

Since life insurance payouts are exempt from taxation and the estate, it's a way to fund a large life insurance policy that your heirs will collect on once you're gone.

Additionally, because life insurance does not become part of the estate and go to probate, it is not a matter of public record. So people who want privacy (such as leaving money to a lover or illegitimate child) may consider one of these policies.

---

[4]https://www.forbes.com/sites/barbaramarquand/2016/06/13/leading-a-rebellion-against-whole-life-insurance/#6f33c9e2453e.

[5]https://www.irs.gov/retirement-plans/plan-participant-employee/retirement-topics-401k-and-profit-sharing-plan-contribution-limits.

Unless you're extremely wealthy or fooling around on the side, you're better off steering clear of these products.

For most people, they are one of the worst financial decisions you can make.

Actions to Take

- If you need life insurance, stick to term life insurance.
- Don't buy whole life or any other cash value life insurance that's disguised as an investment product.
- If you do buy whole life, be damn sure you pay that premium every month; otherwise, you've flushed money down the toilet.
- Don't write books bashing life insurance and annuities. You won't have many friends left.

18

Reverse Mortgages

"Save the fireworks for later... The Fonz has a plan."

– Arthur Fonzarelli

I'm generally not a fan of financial products that are pitched by former TV stars like Henry Winkler and the late Alan Thicke. And it's not because I once had a screaming argument with Alan Thicke (true story).

When financial products need the Fonz or the dad from *Growing Pains* to convince you this is a good idea – it probably isn't.

That being said, a reverse mortgage can be a lifeline to desperate seniors who are running out of money.

Like a Mortgage But in Reverse

When you buy a home and take out a mortgage, you borrow money, interest accrues every month, and you make monthly payments.

A reverse mortgage is kind of the opposite of that.

You already own the house, the bank gives you the money up front, interest accrues every month, and the loan isn't paid back until you pass away or move out of the house.

If you die, you never pay back the loan. Your estate does. And your estate won't have to pay more than the value of the house.

So if you owe $300,000 and the value of your house falls to $250,000, your heirs won't be on the hook for the other $50,000.

When you take out a reverse mortgage, you can take the money as a lump sum or as a line of credit anytime you want.

Sweet deal, right?

Wrong.

Reverse mortgages are horrible products that gouge consumers, as I'll explain shortly. Sure, they can help you if you're truly desperate and have no other way to get your hands on some cash. Like I say about annuities and whole life insurance – reverse mortgages aren't wrong for everyone. Just almost everyone.

To meet the requirements before being approved for a reverse mortgage, you must:

- Be 62 years old or older
- Have lived in your home for 12 months or longer
- Have a significant amount of equity in the home
- Meet with an independent government-approved housing counselor

Say what now?

Those first three requirements seem to make sense.

But how dangerous is this product that before you can use it, *the government makes you meet with someone to make sure you really understand what you're getting yourself into?*

I don't recall the government asking borrowers to meet with counselors before taking out interest-only mortgages, obtaining credit cards with 26% interest rates, or applying for auto loans on cars they can't afford.

Clearly, this product is so bad that the government is saying to you, "Are you sure you want to do this? No, I mean are you really, really sure?"

The Most Expensive Loan You'll Ever Find

The way the Fonz makes it sound, you simply tap into the equity in your home, get a six-figure check, and live out your golden years the way you've always dreamed.

But the fact is reverse mortgages are exorbitantly expensive loans.

Like a regular mortgage, you'll pay various fees and closing costs that will total thousands of dollars.

Additionally, you'll pay a mortgage insurance premium.

With a regular mortgage, you can avoid paying for mortgage insurance if your down payment is 20% or more of the purchase price. Since you're not making a down payment on a reverse mortgage, you pay the premium on mortgage insurance.

The premium equals 0.5% if you take out a loan equal to 60% or less of the appraised value of the home. The premium jumps to a whopping 2.5% if the loan totals more than 60% of the home's value.

If your home is appraised at $450,000 and you take out a $300,000 reverse mortgage, it will cost you an additional $7,500 on top of all of the other closing costs.

But wait, we're not done yet.

You'll also get charged roughly $30 to $35 per month as a service fee. The total is charged based on your life expectancy. If you are expected to live another 10 years (120 months) you'll be charged another $3,600 to $4,200. That figure will be deducted from the amount you receive.

Most of the fees and expenses can be rolled into the loan, which means they compound over time.

And this is an important distinction between a regular mortgage and reverse mortgage. When you make payments on a regular mortgage each month, you are paying down interest and principal, reducing the amount you owe.

Because you never write a check to pay down your reverse mortgage, the figure compounds month after month. A regular mortgage compounds on a lower figure each month. A reverse mortgage compounds on a higher number.

Settling Up

The loan is settled when one of two events occur: You (or your surviving spouse if he or she is named on the loan) die, or you move out of your house.

If you pass away, your estate pays back the loan with the proceeds from the sale of your house. If one of your heirs wants to live in the house (even if they already do), they will have to find the money to pay back the reverse mortgage; otherwise, they have to sell the home to pay back the loan.

The other trigger is that you move out of the home. You may decide to relocate to be closer to your children, move in with your kids, or – as expected in the case of one out of every three baby boomers – move to an assisted living facility.

Once you move out, you have a year to close the loan.

What is very scary about the scenario involving nursing homes is they are very expensive.

In 2016, the average cost of a nursing home was $81,128 per year for a semiprivate room.[1] And that figure is likely to rise every year.

Chances are, you'll need the equity in your home to pay some or all of those costs.

If you owe a lender a substantial piece of the equity in your home, there won't be much left for the nursing home. In that case, unless your kids step up to pay for it, you're going to a Medicaid facility, which is something you probably want to avoid.

Lastly, the terms of the loan dictate you must maintain the home and pay all taxes.

So even if you were thinking, "Screw it, I'll let my heirs or the lender worry about fixing up the house and the taxes after I'm gone," you're dead wrong. You could be foreclosed on if you refuse to pay for those things.

If you're truly desperate for cash and have no other alternatives, a reverse mortgage can be a lifeline.

However, the high costs are not worth it for most people. You're better off selling your home and moving to a cheaper place, keeping whatever equity you have in your pocket rather than owing it to a reverse mortgage lender.

Actions to Take

- Only take out a reverse mortgage if you are desperate for cash and have no other sources.
- These are complicated transactions. Be sure you understand exactly what you'll receive and what will be owed.
- If someone lives in the house with you, be certain they have a backup plan for when you die or move out. Otherwise, they could be out on the street.
- Don't trust the Fonz. He's not as cool as he used to be.

---

[1] https://longtermcare.acl.gov/costs-how-to-pay/costs-of-care.html.

Conclusion

"This is the end"

– The Doors

So that's it.

I hope *You Don't Have to Drive an Uber in Retirement* provided you with plenty of income generating ideas, cost cutting measures, and reasons why you should stay away from popular strategies that make other people money, but not you.

Using just a few of the methods in this book should easily add a few hundred to a few thousand dollars per month in income and savings.

Take back control of your retirement. Let me know how these strategies work for you. I'd love to hear about your success in preparing for retirement or how these ideas are working for you in retirement. If you made extra money or saved a bunch of cash, send me the details.

You can email me at feedback@uberretirementbook.com. Please note, while I cannot provide personal advice, I'm always writing about retirement issues and ways to generate income on my free website, www.wealthyretirement.com.

You can also learn about which specific Perpetual Dividend Raising stocks I'm recommending by subscribing to *The Oxford Income Letter*. As a reader of this book, you'll get an extra $10 off the already discounted price.

Visit www.uberretirementbook.com/incomeletter for details.

Here's to being in control of your retirement,

Marc

About the Author

Marc Lichtenfeld is the Chief Income Strategist of the Oxford Club and editor of *The Oxford Income Letter*. He also runs several Oxford Club VIP trading services. He is the author of the best seller *Get Rich with Dividends*, which has been published in several languages. He has appeared on CNBC, Fox Business, Bloomberg, and National Public Radio, and his work has been featured on WSJ.com and in *U.S. News and World Report, Business Insider,* and many other publications.

Highly sought after, Marc regularly speaks at investment conferences all over the world.

Marc is a former Wall Street analyst and journalist. He is the only published financial analyst to serve as a ring announcer for world championship boxing and mixed martial arts on HBO, Showtime, and ESPN.

Acknowledgments

This book would not be in your hands without the help of a lot of people.

Thank you to Tula Weis, formerly of Wiley, who believed in this book from the beginning; Michael Henton of Wiley for picking up where Tula left off; also from Wiley, Judy Howarth, who edited *Get Rich with Dividends* and played a big part in the publishing of this book; Stewart Smith for your helpful edits, Emily Paul and Caroline Maria Vincent for all of your help; and Jean-Karl Martin for helping make the world aware of this book.

Dr. Mark Skousen, thank you for lending your wisdom and gravitas to this project.

To my friends and colleagues at Agora and The Oxford Club, it is a pleasure and honor to work with you every day.

Julia Guth, thank you doesn't begin to express my gratitude. This book and other projects would not have seen the light of day without your support and confidence.

Bill Bonner, Mark Ford, and Myles Norin, the company Bill and Mark started and that Myles runs is a special place. Thank you for creating an environment that encourages employees to thrive.

Alexander Green, I greatly appreciate your support over the past ten years. You've set the bar very high, and I work hard every day to try to match your level of excellence. Karim Rahemtulla, for giving me my start at The Oxford Club, your friendship, and for a lot of amazing dinners.

To my fellow Oxford Club editors, Matt Carr, Steve McDonald, Andy Gordon, Adam Sharp, Eric Fry, Andy Snyder, and Dave Fessler – I can't think of a smarter, more interesting group that I'd rather share ideas with and argue about whether crypto is in a bubble.

Jennifer Lawrence, for always being a champion for my books and other projects.

Chad Barrett, Chris Witmer, Heidi "Cuz" Barboy, and the rest of the marketing team for helping to get the word out.

My former managing editors, Alex Moschina, Mike Kapsch, Patrick Little, and Colleen Hill. Your feedback and hard work were invaluable in making the *Oxford Income Letter* what it is today. Your influence is seen throughout this book.

Kristin Orman, I still can't believe my good fortune that you were available and in South Florida again after a nine-year break. I'm glad we remained friends all those years and am thrilled that we work side by side every day.

Rachel Gearhart, the wait was worth it. Thank you for pouring your heart and soul into everything and being the incredible editor and friend that you are. I hope my writing doesn't force you to work *more than* 10 hours a day.

Mom and Dad, thank you for all that you've given me over the years.

Eric, for your advice when writing was (is) a struggle. As Charlie Babbitt said, "I like having you for my brother."

Julian and Kira, words cannot express how proud I am to be your father. I hope this book is something you'll look back on and be proud to be my son and daughter.

Holly, there is no chance my journey would be as successful, fun, and happy without you. I don't know how I could possibly deserve you, but I am thankful everyday that you called me early that Tuesday morning.

Index